MW01200086

JULIO IGLESIAS

JULIO IGLESIAS

MARSHA DALY

ST. MARTIN'S PRESS / NEW YORK

Library of Congress Cataloging in Publication Data

Daly, Marsha.
Julio Iglesias.

1. Iglesias, Julio, 1943– . 2. Singers—Spain—
Biography. I. Title.
ML420.I35D3   1986   784.5′0092′4 [B]   85-26071
ISBN 0-312-44853-8

Design by Victoria Hartman

First Edition

10 9 8 7 6 5 4 3 2 1

To
Morton Tuller
with my thanks for all his help

ACKNOWLEDGMENTS

If there is one person who made the completion of this book possible, it is Miriam Fernández Soberón, entertainment editor of the Spanish-language newspaper *Noticias del Mundo*. Her research and background information on Julio's life were indispensable to the project.

I would also like to acknowledge the assistance of Edna Gillim and Debbie Herschaft in opening the files of Sterling's Magazines to me.

JULIO IGLESIAS

*C*an 500 million women be wrong? The superstar singer Julio Iglesias, often called the Spanish Sinatra, just happens to claim that round figure as his fans around the world. Is it just hype? No, because Iglesias can back up his boasts with facts.

Fact: He has given more than two thousand live concerts in his seventeen-year career, to standing-room-only crowds on all six continents.

Fact: He has appeared on more than eight hundred television programs in sixty-nine countries, usually as the host.

Fact: He records in seven languages to please his fans— Spanish, German, Japanese, Italian, French, Portuguese, and English.

Fact: He has collected at last count 221 platinum records and 680 gold records as proof of his sales power. At last count his album sales had topped the 110 million mark.

And yet, for all that, just three years ago one of the biggest jokes on TV was the question, "Julio who?"—the result of a high-powered publicity campaign that kept his name in the news before he had any American product to back it up.

At the time, he was an international recording star with those above-mentioned impressive statistics, but the one market he most coveted, the United States of America, still shimmered before him, an alluring but elusive goal. He referred to this market as "the Saxons" to differentiate it from his primary audience, the Hispanics. America was the challenge he could not resist, maybe because he has thrived on battling impossible odds—and beating them. He had done it in his personal life and was sure he could repeat it professionally.

When he finally launched his first English-language records, in 1984, he did indeed triumph. His album *1100 Bel Air Place* was a million seller within three weeks of its release. Three singles from the LP all earned Julio more gold records. The success of this one project made him one of America's biggest money-makers in 1984.

As *People* magazine reported in its survey of top earners that year, "Julio Iglesias earned $4.6 million for *1100 Bel Air Place.* He also made $1.7 million gross from 10 sellout concerts in the U.S."

By the end of 1984 no one was asking "Julio who?" anymore, and his fan club swelled with a few million American women who were captivated by this sexy, handsome hunk of a singer. They wanted to know more about him.

In the U.S. that doesn't mean just knowing about his singing career. When American women adopt an idol, they demand to know everything about him, from the loves in his life, to the color of his underwear, to what he wears to bed. But in spite of his international superstardom and his phenomenal fame on American pop charts, Julio Iglesias seems intentionally to avoid the usual media outlets hot new personalities seek—women's magazines, the local talk show circuit. This sex symbol has been highly selective when it comes to talking to his American audience.

Oddly, this reaction to his newfound fame was in direct contrast to his attempts to become a household name in the States. He mounted one of the most expensive public relations campaigns ever in show business to launch his career here. To many students of publicity, the packaging of Julio Iglesias has gone down as a classic campaign. It was worth every penny, because it worked. However, to many, Julio remains a man of mystery, ever eager and ready to talk about his music, his career, and his success, but just as reluctant to reveal details about the other side —his personal life.

While researching this book, I came to sense that there are really two different Julio Iglesiases: the extravagant, elegant, gallant, spotlight-loving entertainer and the quiet, retiring, shy multimillionaire who prefers solitude or the company of his family and an extremely small group of trusted associates to the crowds that surround him in public. He seems comfortable with both sides, but there is also a trace of sadness in a man who admits, "I have many houses, but no home."

The better-known Iglesias is the one who excites audiences around the globe. When he takes center stage, Julio exudes a sense of sexual fire caged inside his nearly six-foot-tall, muscular, athletic body. And as he sings his well-polished love songs into the microphone, he unleashes a powerful sensuality, enhancing the romantic ballads that have become his trademark. Hispanic female fans have been known to swoon in their seats during his concerts, very much the way Frank Sinatra affected American women in the 1940s.

And yet, offstage, when this aspect of his talent is raised, he refuses to concede that his popularity may be based on a strong sexual attraction. If anything, he seems embarrassed by the notion that he is considered a sex symbol; he places the emphasis on his hard-earned singing style instead, and claims that he purposefully avoids the stage tactics that other musical superstars employ to incite their fans. Julio sees himself as "a man who loves women, life, the sun, sports, and my solitude. Onstage I don't dance around or jump up and down. I don't use my body to manipulate people."

To a good degree, the two distinct personalities have been able to reconcile themselves in the singer, but he is learning that "the Saxons" continue to demand to know more about his offstage life, and if denied this hobby of prying into their idols' private lives, they can turn fickle and point their attentions elsewhere.

And precisely because much of the media considers him a star packaged or created by a high-powered publicity program, the jury is still out as to his staying power in America. However, Julio's fame does not rest on America. Internationally no other single star has ever achieved his level of success and remained at that level for so long. His is truly a remarkable story, full of tragedy and triumph, and, in more ways than one, it is a blueprint for other aspiring artists to follow.

·1·

Born with a Silver Spoon

*I*t is rare for a man of Julio Iglesias' background to end up on the pinnacle of show business. His childhood was, unlike those of most show business successes, very full of advantages. If there ever was a book called "Lives of the Great Superstars," the one thread that would run as a common bond through their stories would be the lack of money in their families. The majority of famous singers rose from the ranks of the poor or lower-middle class.

Frank Sinatra's parents lavished love on their only child and he wanted for little, but he still learned about life as a street kid in Hoboken, New Jersey. Elvis's parents were unskilled laborers who raised their only child in shacks and public housing projects. In Britain the Beatles all came from working-class homes, as did Tom Jones. Their backgrounds provided strong psychological motives that helped speed them onward, as did unusual looks, gangly bodies, and a host of insecurities that come from feeling "different."

It was their talent that gave many of these future stars their first acceptance with peers. And it was their talent that opened a door to opportunity denied others in their family or social circumstances. Once at the top, they rarely looked back, and, except for waxing nostalgic to reporters about the now often whitewashed good old days, they have rarely gone home again.

Julio Iglesias is the exception; he quite frankly entered life with a silver spoon in his mouth. He was born Julio José Iglesias de la Cueva on September 23, 1943. His father, Dr. Julio Iglesias Puga, was descended from one of the oldest families in Spain, a true blue blood. His mother, María del Rosario de la Cueva Perignat, had her roots in the district of Andalusia.

Dr. Iglesias Puga was already a well-established gynecologist when Julio was born, and the family was living in Spain's capital, Madrid. At the time, Spain was still struggling for an identity. Ravaged by a bitter civil war that split the country between liberal Republicans and the conservative Falangists, Spain was then in the political hands of Generalissimo Francisco Franco, who had led the Falangists to victory. Although there was burdensome repression under Franco, the Spaniards were relieved to end the war that, like the American Civil War, had pitted brother against brother. After the uneasy peace that came in 1939, the country was slowly putting its economic house in order, and Franco was trying to heal old wounds.

But the year of Julio's birth, 1943, was not a very prosperous one anywhere in the world. While Spain was trying to piece itself back together, World War II broke out in Europe and the Pacific. Franco would keep Spain officially neutral for the duration, but his sympathies, unlike those of neighboring Portugal, were clearly with the fascist Axis powers. Italy and Germany had given him strong support in the 1936–39 civil war, while many Americans had fought with the Republicans, whose supporters were identified as leftist.

Franco, however, was a pragmatic leader, and with little fanfare or visible regret he smoothly switched sides as it became apparent that the Allies would be victorious. Thus he assured that his countrymen would suffer no permanent damage from his minor political lapses.

Because Franco was able to walk deftly the thin line between the warring factions, Spain was able to supply itself with necessary commodities through the war years. Certainly the war did not seem to touch the Iglesias family, nor did the poverty that was also indigenous to Spain.

Julio's memories of his childhood are happy ones. The Iglesias home was spacious and in one of Madrid's finest neighborhoods, close to the Parque del Oeste. A couple of years later his brother, Carlos, arrived to complete the family. Dr. Iglesias cut a handsome figure after the war when he and his family took regular Sunday strolls through the park. Because of his medical reputation, the doctor was well known, but he seemed to avoid the political cliques many of his fellow aristocrats joined.

The family was extremely well-to-do, but they lived comfortably, not ostentatiously. Dr. Iglesias never let his thriving medical practice interfere with his fatherly duties, and he formed an especially close relationship with his firstborn, Julio. Whenever Julio reflects on his early years, his thoughts always turn to his father. "With my father," he has said, "my childhood was wonderful. He was good, simply good. And he was always present."

Dr. and Mrs. Iglesias, of course, occupied a high position in Madrid, where money and family name can mean the difference between traveling in the fast lane with the powerful and standing still. Dr. Iglesias was never one to stand still, a trait he passed along to both his sons. Competition was keen in the family, and the boys were taught always to strive for the best, to be at the top.

Julio and Carlos were the center of the household, the apples of their parents' eyes. While neither their mother nor their father believed in spoiling the children, just their station in life made the boys confident about their futures. It was only natural that, growing up in a loving home, surrounded by servants and the best of everything, Julio would look at the world with optimism.

Spain, a poor but proud nation, was rich in a cultural heritage that rivaled the best in Europe. Under the conservative leadership of Franco, it was clinging to Old World ways. Officially, it was a republic, with opportunity for people from all walks of life. In truth, socially and economically, it was still tied to a rigid social stratification ruled by the aristocracy.

It certainly helped that Julio's family was part of that aristocracy. He attended the best schools—Catholic, of course, since Spain was officially bound to the Roman Catholic Church. In the aristocracy there was another tradition —the parents of children of that class chose careers for their children. With their money and name, Julio's parents could take their pick of professions and know that, because of his heritage alone, Julio was assured of success.

With Julio, the choice was easy. Slender, with dark, intense good looks and a natural charm from the day he was born, the boy clearly was destined for a career working with people. Early on, his parents decided to groom him for the diplomatic service, and it was plausible that young Julio would one day be Spain's ambassador to one of the important world embassies—France, Britain, or the United States.

As a dutiful son, Julio would never rebel against his parents' wishes. But on the other hand, he did not apply himself in school, choosing to get by on his quick intelligence rather than working hard to earn good grades. As he progressed through his school, Sagrado Corazón, it was obvious that he was not really academically inclined. His parents made every effort to get him to study, to live up to his potential, but his big interest was sports, not books. After his parents, Julio's first love was soccer. To Europeans, soccer is as important as baseball and football together are to people in the U.S.; it is the number-one sport everywhere except in the United States. It is also one of the most rugged, played at full running speed with few breaks and fewer substitutions. Undoubtedly, it was his early athletic training in soccer that helped Julio later in life when he could draw out a musical note to incredible lengths and keep absolute control of its tone and pitch.

That, of course, was not even on his mind as he spent long hours on his athletic skills, building up his wind and his leg muscles. Back then, Spanish schoolboys set their sights on professional soccer. Julio, playing his heart out for school teams, yearned to be one of the best, eventually to earn a spot on Spain's top team, Real Madrid.

Julio was one of their most devoted fans. In 1956, when he was thirteen years old, he watched Madrid go wild over Real Madrid's winning of the European Champions Cup, and he wanted more than ever to play on the team. What made him outstanding in sports was his strong competitive drive, a trait that would have ensured him success in whatever he chose to do.

His parents, especially his father, were enthusiastic about his soccer ability, but they urged him to continue his studies and to pursue other interests. María Iglesias was happy when Julio expressed an interest in music. Like most teenagers, he was up-to-date on the latest pop songs, which on Spain's hit parade meant Spanish, Mexican, and American singers, but he had a taste for classical music as well.

The Iglesiases first became aware of Julio's musical talent at his grandmother's house. She had a beautiful grand piano, and as soon as Julio could reach the keyboard, he enjoyed sitting down and picking out tunes, often making them up as he went along. Music, however, was merely a pleasant hobby to him, and he felt no urge to perform publicly.

Every summer the boys escaped the city heat with trips to the seaside, to their father's ancestral homeland, Galicia. Spain is a country fragmented into several strongly divided provinces, many of whose inhabitants vow greater allegiance to their special homeland than to Spain itself. Chief among these divisions are the Castilians, Valencians, Andalusians, Asturians, Catalans, Galicians, and Basques. The Basques are the most zealously chauvinistic in their separatist claims. Each state has its own language or dialect.

Dr. Iglesias hails from a long line of Galicians in northwestern Spain. To the Spanish, Galicia is the cultural heart of the country. It was often said that to write poetry in Spain was to write in Galicia. Later, remembering his summers playing on the beaches and swimming in the warm, welcoming waters of this mystical homeland, Julio would write "Canto a Galicia," as much to honor his intense emotional bond with his father as the land itself.

But there can be no doubt that the hauntingly beautiful song springs from his father's deep attachment to Galicia. Even decades after Galicians leave the lush green hills and mountains and forests behind, they still feel the pull of what Galicians call *morriña,* a yearning or homesickness that has been likened to the blues made famous by American blacks. Galicians leave home only because of grinding poverty and lack of opportunity, but a part of their heart always stays behind.

During the school year, of course, Julio and Carlos lived in Madrid and concentrated on their schoolwork and friends. Julio got along well with everyone, so despite his mediocre grades, it was certain that he would go on to law school and then into the diplomatic service as planned. As long as he could play soccer, Julio did not worry about his future.

There were so few disappointments, so much fun and good times that to this day Julio recalls his childhood in the most glowing terms. His only setback came when he wanted to join the choir at Sagrado Corazón. It was one of the best choirs in the city, and Julio, ever seeking new challenges, aspired to sing in it. His voice was considered quite good, but there was a grade requirement that kept him out. Back then the rejection hurt. Today, considering his vocal success, he can enjoy the irony. And it had no lasting effect on him. He says now, "I dream for my children a youth like the one I had. So many years of good fortune."

He also excelled in one other area, one which would stand him in good stead in the foreign service. He had a good ear for foreign languages, most specifically French, which then was the universal diplomatic language. And so, when he graduated from high school, he agreeably went along with his parents' desire for his career. After all, he had no better suggestion; the diplomatic service was a profession that would allow him to travel and was prestigious enough to impress his friends and girl friends, most notably the latter!

Julio was always attractive to the opposite sex; he never had trouble getting dates. He discovered that women seemed to gravitate more to athletes than to studious types, and in addition to his superior athletic skills, he was exceptionally good-looking. Women liked his quick, sunny smile and enjoyed his company.

After graduation from high school Julio indicated that he was willing to continue his education—but he wanted to try out for a soccer career first. The yearly competition for Real Madrid is fierce; young men from the four corners of

Spain compete in the annual trials. Julio had never before been involved in such a struggle, one where his family and money could not help. He would have to earn a place on his talent alone.

Julio proved worthy; he played his way onto Real Madrid's junior team, an amateur club that seasons the athletes for the tough professional league. This had been his first real dream, and it was coming true. Nothing could stand in his way, and with international sports stardom under his belt, he looked forward to the foreign service.

Just nineteen, he was on top of the world, a goalie for Real Madrid's farm team, a son who was making his father proud. It seemed he could do no wrong. Then fate intervened. From a youth with limitless possibilities before him, Julio was suddenly and violently thrown into a nightmare world where he came face to face with death.

·2·

Death and Rebirth

*T*ragedy struck in July 1963, on what started out as just another ordinary night. Julio was behind the wheel of his sports car, on his way to a Madrid stadium for a soccer match. As he was driving down the highway, a freak one-in-a-million accident happened; without any warning one of the wheels flew off his convertible, spinning the car out of control. The car flipped over and over until it was just a twisted wreck. To this day, those who witnessed the accident and the car afterward believe that only a miracle saved Julio's life. And for a long while that miracle was itself touch-and-go.

When the emergency team arrived, they immediately tried to free the driver's shattered body from the wreckage. At first they did not think he was alive, and from his apparent injuries, little hope was held out that he would live out the night. Thousands of shards of glass had sprayed over him, leaving his face a blood-covered mask. His body had suffered multiple fractures.

For the next fourteen hours Julio lay on an operating table in the hospital as doctors raced against time to piece him together again. All the family, including his physician father, could do was wait and pray.

Julio survived the crisis period, and the Iglesiases rejoiced. But although the surgery was successful in terms of life and death, there were complications beyond a surgeon's skills. Julio would be bound to a wheelchair. According to his doctors, injury to his spine had caused a compression that was diagnosed incurable—he would never walk again.

It was a terrible blow. Stunned, Julio realized that he would never walk on the beach again, never play soccer again. He was paralyzed from the waist down. When the full impact of his situation hit him, Julio sank into a deep depression.

A few weeks later he passed his twentieth birthday, flat on his back in the hospital, covered with bandages, a heavy cast weighing down his body. The change in fortune had been too swift. Suddenly, after being one of life's golden gods, he was in despair, afraid he would accomplish nothing and be a burden on his family.

In the first desperate months after the crash, as he struggled with pain and the shock of the tragedy, Julio believed what the doctors were saying. But as his body healed, the old fighting spirit returned. He had never been a quitter, and from somewhere deep within his mind, he found the courage to battle his way back. His enemy, he realized, was now not his body but his mental state.

It has never been possible to come up with a formula to explain why certain rare individuals are able to overcome severe physical handicaps, even paralysis, while the majority accept their circumstances. Perhaps it is due to an inner drive too powerful to thwart. Whatever the reasons, the same intense concentration that enabled Julio to make Real Madrid's junior team he applied to getting out of that wheelchair. "I was paralyzed," he has said, "but from the bed I started to renew my life."

The process of renewal was slow and painful. After having been bedridden for so long, he had to retrain other parts of his body back to their normal strength, not just his legs. In the months after the operation his forced inactivity sent his weight plummeting from his usual robust, athletic 190 pounds to less than 100. He had "no flesh, no muscles," he explains. "But my mind was strong like a bull. And it is the mind that moves the muscles."

Julio actually willed himself out of his wheelchair. He refused to accept a life sentence. And as he set new goals for each day, goals that would return him to the active, fun-filled life he had once taken for granted, he had time to do a lot of thinking. So much had been handed to him on a silver platter. Now he had to work to get it back.

He was grateful to be given a second chance. Through the years he has spent many hours thinking about the gift of new life he was given. With a smile and a shrug he has said, "At twenty you just want to go through life," until something happens to make you appreciate life more. "To fight for life makes you see something you would never see," he adds. "After the accident everything was, Why?"

Most of the whys centered in his survival—and his lingering paralysis. Why should he accept the doctors' verdict? Why couldn't he at least rebuild his atrophied muscles and try to walk again? At that moment he had no answers, but he knew it would cost him nothing to try.

Once his bones had mended, Julio set a tough schedule for himself: exercise to regain his muscle tone and, he secretly believed, the use of his legs. His stamina and tenacity amazed the hospital staff. After months of disuse, when he began his program he was in great physical pain, but he never pampered himself. Every day he worked to stretch just a little more than he had the day before.

His doctors were afraid he was doing too much, but Julio was never satisfied. When he could not use the hospital's physical therapy room, he worked out on equipment his family had installed at his request in his room. If anyone believed in his rehabilitation as much as Julio, it was Dr. Iglesias. To speed his progress, Julio dragged himself to the equipment even at night and went through the exercises again and again.

His determination was regarded as an inspiration in the hospital. That iron-willed spirit coupled with the Iglesias wit and charm drew others to him, especially the young nurses. Instead of being bitter, angry, and dependent, Julio maintained a lighthearted attitude, and his spontaneous warmth helped cheer up others. Perhaps it was at this crucial period that Julio's real personality emerged. He is what the Spanish call *chistoso*, which means gracefully amusing and taking nothing seriously. And, indeed, Julio does exaggerate outrageously, an attitude he developed during his long convalescence.

Because he was a hospital favorite, the nurses were always trying to find new interests for Julio. Since he would never be able to play soccer again with his old skill, one nurse, aware of his musical talent, presented him with an old guitar someone was about to throw away. Julio was delighted. The strumming was excellent therapy for his hands and arms, and idly composing little tunes was a pleasant respite from his physical exercise.

At first he did not take music seriously. Once back on his feet, he planned to return to school, get a law degree, and follow through on his family's desire to see him go into the diplomatic service. Singing was a hobby in his family, not a profession.

Julio's physical progress the first year after the accident was painfully slow. His bones had mended and his face healed, although anyone looking closely at him can see to this day the many tiny scars the shattered glass left on his face; his deep tan helps to hide the evidence. But the spinal injury still left him chairbound.

Other patients might have lost hope after a year of difficult rehabilitation work, but Julio merely drove himself harder. Then the miracle happened. One day he realized that feeling was returning to his feet. That was the only sign he needed to make him redouble his efforts. It was just a question of time, he believed, until he left his wheelchair for good.

It took him two years to recuperate fully from the car crash, but he ultimately regained total use of his legs. Once he took his first tentative steps, his strength increased, and soon he was swimming and even running again.

The accident, however, had deprived him of two of the years that are crucial to a young man's future. The family plans for him had suffered a severe setback. Julio put aside his guitar and turned his thoughts to preparing for the foreign service. His parents wanted him to learn English, an important second language for anyone entering the diplomatic corps, and they were sending him to Cambridge, England, to study. (Somehow, over the years, the fact that Julio studied language in Cambridge has led to the mistaken notion that he took his law degree from that city's most prestigious institution, Cambridge University. Actually, he later returned home to Madrid to enter law school.) Somehow, though, the guitar wound up in his luggage; it was as if fate would not let him forget that music was now a part of his life.

Naturally, Julio believed it was still just a means to escape the intensity of his studies. As he says, "If in 1966 you say to me I'm going to be a singer, I can't believe it. Not ever. But people don't know what they have inside until they discover it one day."

Meanwhile, he was already jotting down the love songs that had so captivated the nurses in the hospital. They were the first to encourage Julio's talent, even suggesting that he send some of his compositions to publishers and recording companies in Spain. He did submit several, but he was not very much surprised to get them back. Despite his well-connected family, he faced the same roadblocks as anyone else breaking into show business, one of the toughest professions for novices. Rejection is part of the territory, and since Julio was not depending on songwriting for his livelihood, he took it in stride.

What he really wanted to do was make up for all the time he had lost when he had been paralyzed. He delighted in his newfound freedom at Cambridge. While there Julio mingled with the university students in the local pubs where he enjoyed pursuing his favorite hobbies—women and song. At Cambridge he met beautiful girls from all over Europe, and he met many more in his travels around the Continent. Almost immediately Julio made up for his long confinement, discovering a deep affinity for the bachelor's life.

Between school and his swinging social schedule, Julio should not have found time for music. But no matter what he was doing, he could not tune out the melodies running through his head. When he should have been studying, more often than not he was strumming his guitar and writing songs.

He did his best to cover up his growing interest in music. For his family's sake, he continued his studies, but now it was just out of a sense of duty. He had to admit to himself that music was his greatest love. The question was, How could he explain this development to his mother and father?

If asked, Julio could not pinpoint the moment he made up his mind to be an entertainer. Certainly the desire had been there for a long time, but it had been dormant throughout his childhood. "When you are a young child," he explains, "you dream about impossible things. When you are twenty years old, you start to dream with your eyes open." With his eyes wide open, Julio could no longer hide the truth from anyone: he wanted to express himself through his music.

Naturally, he had his doubts about switching from something as secure as law to entertainment, but he was reassured by friends who regarded his talents highly. Julio contends it was those friends who sealed his fate as a performer. "You write the music and the lyrics, and people say yes, and that is the moment it all happens," he says.

His decision to be an entertainer was not a frivolous one. If he had this undeniable talent, it was his responsibility to share it with the world. And he has always believed his musical abilities are a blessing, "a gift, not a technique; it's something that doesn't belong to me because I fight for it, but it's a gift that must be developed. But without the gift you can't develop anything," he adds.

Many cultures harbor an innate feeling that supernatural or otherworldly forces are at work in nature that shape people's destinies. Although Julio Iglesias is a sane, rational man, he believes in these mystical powers. If salt is spilled on the table, he will leave; if he hears bad news, he burns the clothes he was wearing when he heard it, including his underwear and socks, and he never forgets to knock on wood before going onstage. Americans would dismiss such superstitions as old wives' tales, leftovers from our ancestors' Old World ways. But it should be remembered that this is precisely the type of upbringing Julio had, an old-fashioned childhood in what is considered part of the Old World—Spain.

His father undoubtedly thought composing was just a passing phase for his son, but he was used to indulging his children. It was okay for Julio to pursue his interest in music—as long as he promised to complete his education, which would give him a real career to fall back on if he failed as an entertainer.

The deal was fair, so Julio agreed to attend law school

while he sent his songs to recording companies. Song after song was returned, but Julio refused to quit. Finally one director at a big company returned his latest effort with a good word and supportive advice. He liked Julio's demo record and urged him to sing his own songs, suggesting that he enter local song contests. The contests had launched many European artists; they were a traditional way to break into show business. Most of the recording companies sent representatives to the contests to scout upcoming singers and songwriters.

At this man's suggestion, Julio entered the Benidorm Song Festival, an annual event open to novices. It was a summer competition, so it would not interfere with school. The problem was, Julio entered at the last minute and left himself practically no time to prepare. Never having sung in public before, he felt awkward and terribly inexperienced when he got to Benidorm and realized how sophisticated his competition was.

The smart move would have been to quit the contest, gain some real performing experience, and come back again next year. Once again, though, his competitive drive calmed his nerves as he walked onstage. A complete unknown, he was given no chance of winning. Even the luck of the draw went against him, as he was to be the first singer to perform. It was a hot July night when Julio took center stage for the first time.

His song was simple, autobiographical, and it was apparent from the start that "La Vida Sigue Igual" ("Life Continues All the Same") was written and sung straight from Julio's heart. His clear, vibrant voice brought the song off with unusual authority for such a novice, and there was something about the handsome, slender, intense singer that impressed the festival sponsors and judges. Intent on his performance, Julio was unaware of the electricity his appearance was generating.

When the contest ended a couple of days thereafter, to his total amazement, Julio walked off with first prize. Part of the prize was a contract to record his winning song. Two weeks after it went on sale in Spain, the song hit the top of the charts.

The record changed his life overnight. It was an exhilarating experience, success, a high he had never known before. The first taste of success left Julio hungry for more. If he could climb so high on inexperience, he sensed that with work his progress would be limitless. Now Julio was at peace; music was where he belonged. From now on he would sacrifice a normal life for applause from an audience and rapid record sales.

It wasn't a conscious decision, but Julio well remembers "the first time I heard myself on the radio. I was in a car with my girl friend. I turned to her and said, 'I don't know whether I prefer you or the radio.' " And, indeed, women have taken second place to his career. Even his future wife would lose to Julio's career when she asked him to make the choice.

Spain in the 1960s was a relatively small market for record companies. The top singing stars had to penetrate other Hispanic markets—Mexico, Central and South America—to make a good income. Several of the big American labels, however, were beginning to expand their lists in Spain because the market there promised to grow rapidly.

CBS España expressed interest in Julio, and he did not hesitate to sign with them. It was a match made in heaven. CBS is an aggressive company, sparked by the same spirit of competition that drives Julio. The company was impressed by his restless energy; here was an artist eager to grow, one who could put Spain on the international recording scene.

Julio embarked in 1969 on the hectic pace he would keep up for the next fifteen years. He traveled to Chile for his initial international exposure at the popular Viña del Mar Song Festival and then went on to the Festival of Brassow in Rumania, where he was awarded the Grand Prize. After that, nothing could stop him. For Julio, achievement meant higher record sales, bigger crowds at his concerts; he was insatiable in his thirst for fame. The money that came with it was just a bonus; his family had never had to worry about money. But Julio seemed out to prove he could be the best, most popular singer in the world.

·3·

Troubador to the World

*J*ulio had to prove he was not a one-hit singer.
CBS España was behind him, willing to provide
all the publicity he needed, and it was no secret that Julio
welcomed the trips, the fans, the adulation. But the record
company also handled numerous other singers, and Julio
wanted his own production people. Not even the greatest
stars can shine without the proper showcasing, which is why
they surround themselves with a personal team whose business it is to further their star's career.

Under CBS's guidance, Julio polished a batch of new
songs, which the company wanted him to record for an
album. This brought him back to England. London, still
celebrating the explosive success of the Beatles, the Rolling
Stones, and other rock superstars, was a major recording
center, home of the most modern facilities in Europe.

Maybe it was a case of wishful thinking on CBS Records'
or Julio's part, but the studio chosen for his debut album
was the same one the Beatles used to tape their records.
The Decca Studios were considered lucky, and there was
always the hope that some of the Beatles' success would rub
off on other performers.

Ten songs comprised his first long-player, and as soon as
the album was released, Julio introduced the numbers all

over Spain in a tough tour. Already his name was enough to fill the concert halls. But Julio kept tabs on his rivals and decided he had to find an edge if he was to survive in the overcrowded field of singing.

If Julio has outpaced and outlasted the performers who started out with him, it is due to his farsightedness. There were others with better voices, more exciting stage personalities, even better looks, but Julio was the one who planned and plotted, always staying one or two jumps ahead of his audience. And he never rested. Where others might spend a few weeks in the recording studio, Julio spent months, polishing and perfecting each note in every song.

In the late 1960s television was a major medium in Spain, the one that reached the most people. With his dazzling smile and photogenic face, Julio was a natural. On the strength of his few hit records, his managers groomed him to host a series of variety shows. Julio eventually hosted several hundred shows in nearly every Spanish-speaking country. The idea was to present him as an international headliner, and he was surrounded with a generous sprinkling of non-Hispanic guests, including the American artists Lola Falana and the Osmonds.

Julio worked harder than anyone else at his career. Just as he had worked relentlessly in his effort to walk again, he now put the same energy into molding himself as a superstar. He refused to be sidetracked or distracted in any way. The object of every concert, every new record was to outsell and outperform all his rivals.

Never satisfied, hour after hour Julio tirelessly worked to perfect his style. That smooth, sexy song delivery is the result of exhaustive practice. In his concerts every move, as well as every note, has been carefully choreographed. Julio knows how his songs will be received because he knows how to evoke his audiences' sighs, shrieks, and applause.

Dr. Iglesias with his wife and their sons, Julio and Carlos, on a stroll in Madrid. *(IMAPRESS/Pictorial Parade)*

Dr. Iglesias with young Julio in Córdoba in front of the house where the matador Manolete was born. *(IMAPRESS/Pictorial Parade)*

Julio's father kisses his grandchild, held by its mother, Isabel Preisler. *(IMAPRESS/Pictorial Parade)*

Julio Iglesias is known for his intense concentration in performance. *(Anastasia Pantsios/Kaleyediscope/Star File)*

Julio and
Miss Puerto Rico 1976
(John Barrett)

Julio embraces his father,
with whom he has
always had a close
relationship (1981).
(AGIP/Pictorial Parade)

Surrounded by pretty chorus members at the Palais des Congrès after a concert in 1981. *(AGIP/Pictorial Parade)*

Julio and his wax double at the Musée Grévin in 1982. The wax
sculpture was created by Daniel Druet, the museum sculptor.
(*AGIP/Pictorial Parade*)

Even in the earliest phase of his career he sensed that the truly great artists were the ones who packaged themselves in the image the fans wanted. Julio saw himself as a romantic balladeer and thus decided to become the number-one singer of love songs.

One of the results of this decision was the procession of women of all ages who came into his life. Because of their wide public exposure song idols frequently become the objects of their fans' desires. Love is the universal language, after all, so the more talented a performer is, the more his audiences believe the sensual messages emanating from the screen or record or concert stage. Sometimes the combination of strong sexual magnetism with a high-powered publicity campaign creates fan reactions that can go out of control. Frank Sinatra in the 1940s, Elvis in the 1950s, and the Beatles in the 1960s are examples of what can happen when idols are created; at the height of their superstardom all were more like prisoners than pampered stars, afraid to leave their hotels or homes for fear of being torn apart by their fans.

Julio was not seeking that type of stardom, but he was aware of the effect his singing had on women. After all, his style was highly personal, calculated to make every woman in his audience believe he was singing only to her. It was only natural that after every one of his concerts there would be a line of female fans waiting for him at the stage door.

At this stage of his career Julio was still playing the field with women. Singers are often advised not to marry young, as this hurts their image with the fans. It is doubtful that Julio needed this advice, as he was more involved with his music than with women.

Yet even as he sought greater fame, he also thought about starting his own family. He was discovering that "fame isn't a very loyal woman. It's not a permanent love." But even as he matured in his attitude toward women, his schedule was such that he rarely spent more than one night in any town.

For the time being, his career would be his wife and mistress. Shortly after his successful Spanish tour, he returned to Madrid for TV shows and, to his delight, a movie. "La Vida Sigue Igual" had attracted interest from a film producer who was anxious to turn it into a movie. Best of all, since the song was associated with Julio and known to be autobiographical, the singer was asked to play himself in the film. Julio agreed, but as the project progressed, he admitted that there was a special art to appearing at ease before the camera and it was one he had not yet mastered.

After shooting the movie, Julio flew to Guatemala for another concert, but this one was different. Before, he had performed to benefit himself. Now he was expressing another side of his nature, the side that appreciates all the good fortune he has enjoyed from birth and wants to give to others. This concert was for the Red Cross, and it raised funds for Central Americans who had been hard hit by hurricanes and floods in 1969.

Many entertainers beg off from benefits. Benefits can be tiring and wind up costing stars money out of their own pockets. Julio, however, is famous for his generosity. Guatemala was the first in a large number of shows he has given to raise funds for everything from disaster relief, to the fights against cancer, heart disease, and starvation. No matter how hectic his schedule is, he always finds time to squeeze in benefits—his way of saying thanks for his own good life.

CBS's Spanish record label was also busy in 1969, promoting Julio. The San Remo Festival, limited to Italian composers, still offered one of Europe's best international showcases for performers. All the songs had to be performed by two different artists, and the singers came from all over the Continent, and England and America. It was an

honor to be asked to participate, and it was a golden opportunity for CBS to parade Julio's talent and charm before
important people in the record industry. In a way, Julio was
finally functioning as a diplomat, only instead of serving a
country, he was serving a giant corporation.

Success did depend on Julio's acceptance by these important industry executives. Romantic singers were a glut
on the market; dozens of Spanish performers came every
year from Madrid, Majorca, Barcelona, and small country
towns to seek their fortune in show business. Like sports,
entertainment was one of the best careers open to poor,
uneducated youngsters. One could prosper without any
important connections, family money, or education. Talent, perseverance, and luck were all that was needed to
reach the top.

Julio was certainly luckier than most of his competitors.
He had the talent and drive, along with a name that could
open doors and the money to save him from the squalid
little clubs and small-time dates most performers have to
play to support themselves. For all his fortune, though, like
his peers he still needed help in making a really big name
as a singer—a breakout record. That was something money
could not buy.

With thousands of records released every year, an artist
needs a special push to break out of the pack. For unknown European singers, the best launching pad was
Eurovision, the premier music festival that is considered
the number-one event of the year. It brings together the
best songs from the Continent in a competition that also
provides a gathering place for the industry's kingmakers.
Just being selected is a triumph. It became Julio's next
prime target.

Each country holds its own tryouts and finals, sending its
grand prizewinner on to the contest. In 1970 Julio's trip to
the Eurovision festival began in Barcelona, where dozens

of Spanish songwriters were represented, each hoping to
be the official entry from Spain.

Julio labored long on composing the one song he felt
could not lose. Inevitably his entry would be a lilting love
song. One day inspiration hit when he recalled a lovely
French girl he had met and known all too briefly, a girl
named Gwendolyne. Their fleeting love affair had left a
lasting impression on Julio, and he was still haunted by her
memory. Of her he said, "She was one of the most beautiful
women in my life . . . open, charming, typically French, and
very romantic." Out of that relationship came the song
"Gwendolyne," full of the youthful longings he remembered. He dedicated it to her, and there was little doubt
when he finished as to who would win the contest.

But it was one thing to win in Barcelona, another to win
at Eurovision, where the competition was fierce and the
political infighting also fierce. Winning such a competition
is considered a national honor, so it is as much country
vying with country as singer vying with singer at the festival. So keen is the European interest in the contest that the
finals are televised. In 1970 they were beamed to twenty-six
nations with an estimated audience of 400 million, large
enough to make even a seasoned performer nervous.

But if Julio was feeling the stress of such a big moment,
no one could detect it. Standing before this crowd of prominent stars, producers, composers, and businessmen, he
sang his romantic ballad with his usual expertise. His performance was received with enthusiasm, and the song won
a respectable if disappointing tie for fourth place. However, as most industry insiders know, at these competitions
often it is not the best song that wins, but the one that the
unspoken political factors deem "best."

The critic for *Billboard*, the American Bible of the music
industry, was full of praise for Julio's song. He wrote that
"artistically the best song in the contest was France's 'Marie

Blanche' by Guy Bonnet . . . and 'Gwendolyne,' [a] minor-
keyed song patterned on the 'Autumn Leaves' sequence,
which was well sung by Julio Iglesias. . . ."

More importantly, when CBS rushed the record onto the
market, it swiftly rose to the top of the charts throughout
Latin America and most of Europe. As Julio was already
represented by two other records, "Yo Canto" ("I Sing")
and "Tenía una Guitarra" ("I Had a Guitar"), he was considered one of the company's best singers. His film also
went into release and proved popular. Now his family could
no longer question his career choice; he was a firmly established star.

The adulation in his native land was gratifying. But Spain
still was not a primary market for recording stars. Only a
small portion of the population bought records, perhaps
because it was a very poor country, and to sustain themselves singers still had to establish markets in Argentina,
Brazil, the Philippines, Central America, and, most especially, Mexico. None of these are easy audiences, but with
CBS behind him and with his track record for success, Julio
studied each new market the way a smart, winning champion fighter studies his opponents, leaving nothing to
chance.

Julio developed a marketing technique that enabled him
to visualize beyond each hit record, to map out individual
campaigns for each country, since each, despite the common bond of the Spanish language, had its own peculiar
tastes in music and performers. The next phase of the plan
was to make him as popular with the recording field's VIPs,
the businessmen who control the market forces. This was
accomplished at the MIDEM Conference in 1970, the big
industry-wide convention held in Europe. CBS rolled out
the red carpet for its rising star. From the entire roster of
stars, Julio was the one hand-picked to shine for the company. One CBS exec admitted that the label had come to

the conference in Cannes, France, for just three real reasons—to see all their friends, to hype catalogue sales, and "to give strong promotion to Julio Iglesias." The other labels, of course, were also nurturing their hottest singers. Among the more popular artists on hand were Martha and the Vandellas, Jackie De Shannon, Astrud Gilberto, Shirley Bassey, and Joe Cocker. In the midst of all that American soul, rock, and the newest sound, the bossa nova, Julio's love songs were a tremendous success. CBS hosted an expensive gala to introduce him, and Julio charmed the industry leaders and enchanted their wives with his well-polished act. As the CBS team was flying back to Spain, one executive beamed that when it came to promoting Iglesias at MIDEM, "we have succeeded one hundred percent."

Immediately Julio was off on another tour, stopping at the Radio and Television Festival in Luxembourg, since he was moving into TV in a big way. He then embarked on an unprecedented schedule: Julio gave forty-one concerts in forty-one Spanish cities in the space of one month. An ordinary man would have been exhausted after such a trip, but Julio seemed to thrive on the acclaim, the applause, and the work.

Clearly, Julio was a workaholic, a man addicted to his profession. If he has any other obsession, it is the sun; Julio can lie under its rays for hours, and his tan may be as important to him as his singing. He certainly works as hard at keeping it as he does at music.

Without this single-minded devotion to his career, undoubtedly Julio never would have reached his goal—troubadour to the world. His handsome appearance, aristocratic manners, and pleasant voice all were part of his success, but what separates the superstar from the average performer are the sacrifices that are made along the way.

"There are others who sing better," Julio admits when

assessing his show business position. "But the art of singing isn't as important as the art of enchanting." And perfecting that art was Julio's goal, the sole purpose of his
practice and study. It takes plenty of hard work to turn his
act into what looks like an effortless show. It also takes a
high degree of honesty. While Julio cringes at any criticism,
he always listens and learns from it, and no one is harder
on himself as an entertainer than he is.

By late 1970 the dedication was paying big dividends.
Julio Iglesias was hot on the Hispanic concert circuit,
helped by a high-powered publicity machine that made
sure word of his fame spread. Always a shrewd operator,
Julio realized right from his first record that the press
should be courted, as they can make or break a newcomer.
As long as he was accessible, he could pretty much control
what they wrote about him, deftly turning aside questions
that delved too deeply into his personal life. For their part,
the press was happy reporting on his concerts and the
pretty women who passed through his world. The big question, naturally, was, When would this swinging single settle
down with a wife?

Julio also won a lot of press coverage from his presence
at all the "right" affairs and galas. The tall, dark, and handsome star was becoming the darling of society, a group with
whom he was instantly at home. Most performers invited to
meet and mix with royalty admit they often feel awkward,
out of their element, more like a prize on display than a real
friend. But Julio was born into this society and was able to
relax and mingle with such notables as Princess Grace of
Monaco, who became one of his most doting fans after
hearing him sing at a benefit. Another honored guest at the
benefit, the Aga Khan, became a personal friend.

Besides interesting these world leaders, Julio was making
plans to invade yet another country with his love songs, a
country halfway around the world from Spain and with a

culture totally alien to a European—Japan. Fortunately, love is the universal language. When he made his Japanese debut at Expo '70 in Osaka, he found a willing audience. The reception was so overwhelming that Julio promised to return and sing again—in Japanese!

Back in Spain, Julio's success made news, as did his success with women. To his friends, Julio seemed a happy-go-lucky bachelor. He was rarely without a stunning companion, and he gave the impression that marriage would cramp his style with the ladies.

Then he met a dark-haired, very delicate teenager, and for once the charmer was charmed. Julio was captivated by Isabel Preysler from the moment they met, quite by chance, at a party. The petite seventeen year-old was visiting Madrid from her home in the Philippines when a friend, who knew she was an Iglesias fan, invited her to a party being given for Julio. It was an invitation no schoolgirl could turn down. Julio seemed smitten at once by her beauty and maturity.

While in other times and places a romance between a twenty-seven-year-old man and a seventeen-year-old girl might cause talk, in Latin countries such an age difference is considered natural and attracts no attention. It is normal for girls to marry young, and Julio was considered an ideal catch.

Close associates knew it was love, because for once Julio slowed down long enough for serious dating. When he was on tour, he actually missed Isabel, and the Latin lover had to admit that he indeed was in love. When Julio asked Isabel to marry him, undoubtedly it was a dream come true for her. She was marrying not just a wealthy, successful man, but the idol of millions of women.

It was those millions of female fans that Julio kept in mind in planning their wedding. Although he has great affection for the adoring crowds responsible for his success, he knew what could happen if they learned of his marriage plans. It had happened with other superstars, when what they hoped would be a private ceremony turned into a Roman circus. To avoid this complication at his own wedding, Julio was secretive about the plans.

He vetoed Madrid for the ceremony because he was too well known there. Isabel's family was flying in from the Philippines, and he was anxious to please them. Very quietly, he arranged for the wedding to take place in the ancient and historic city of Toledo, immortalized by the artist El Greco. The couple exchanged their vows on January 21, 1971, and almost before the ink was dry on the certificate, Isabel was off on tour with her bridegroom. Isabel got a quick initiation into what life with her husband would be like. They had to be at the Song Festival in Knoffe, Belgium, where Julio helped the Spanish team win the first prize. From there Julio had to perform in Mexico, Panama, and Puerto Rico. Besides the concerts, there were television shows, recording dates, press parties, interviews, and a stream of business activities that occupied Julio and his associates. Later that year he toured Central and South America.

For Isabel, it meant living out of suitcases in hotel suites, as she went with him whenever possible. Surely at first it was a heady experience for a teenager who went overnight from schoolgirl to wife of an international show stopper. It was exciting and fascinating to be an intimate part of the whirl of concerts, parties, and lavish homes that were always open to Julio. The couple were regulars on the guest lists of the rich and famous and powerful world leaders. And despite his hectic schedule, Julio tried to be a tender, caring husband, generous to a fault, an emotional man who expressed his love in many wonderful ways.

But their life-styles were forced to diverge early in the marriage. Just a few weeks after the wedding Isabel gave

Julio the happy news: they were going to have a baby. Julio was delighted about becoming a father, but the prospect gave him an even greater incentive to succeed.

As the child of a happy home himself, Julio was anxious to offer his own children a firm, secure foundation. That meant concentrating even more on his career, pushing himself harder. Unfortunately, that meant more time away from Isabel, who had to stay behind in Madrid for much of her pregnancy.

Of course, they were still so passionately in love that the separations made their reunions sweeter. Certainly Julio had not hidden the fact that his success was based on lots of travel, or the fact that his career had priority until he was at the top of the business. And Isabel had enough to occupy her during his absences, between setting up their Madrid home and preparing for the baby. Besides, what Julio was doing was building security for both of them, and the results were already visible in their life-style. Naturally, as a newlywed, she would have liked more time alone with Julio, without the entourage that seemed in lockstep with him.

The couple's happiness was complete late that year when they welcomed a daughter, whom they called Chaveli, a nickname for Isabel. But not even her birth slowed down Julio. He spent the Christmas and New Year's holidays working and traveling between Mexico and Hong Kong, performing in concert, and laying down tracks for upcoming albums.

If Isabel was bothered by Julio's business demands, she never let on in public, perhaps due to the tradition in Latin countries that wives must never openly speak against their husbands or complain. That does not mean that a wise woman cannot control her man from behind the scenes. As it happens, Julio's chief rival in Spain, the charismatic singer Raphael, was also married, but his wife had extracted a commitment from him before they married that they would never spend more than thirty days apart. And Raphael has always lived up to that prenuptial promise. Whenever they have been apart that long, he arranges to meet her for a brief but meaningful reunion. But Isabel was very young and inexperienced when she married Julio, still at the stage when girls believe love conquers all and can last forever.

Once the baby was born, of course, they could travel together again. Julio was busy promoting himself in Japan, where he recorded his first song in their language. He also pushed heavily into South America. By 1972 he had celebrated selling his first million albums and was acclaimed by CBS España as their number-one artist for sales throughout the world. But he was still running with the pack, still one in a crowded field of Spanish singers, still competing to be the leader, the first to achieve worldwide recognition.

With that end in sight, Julio pressed on into North Africa and the Middle East, adding new bases to his well-structured, carefully packaged career. When his love songs found acceptance in Germany, he responded by learning the language and recording his first LP in German.

His greatest strength, however, was in South America. At one point his record sales in Chile represented more than 50 percent of that country's national sales, a phenomenal figure. Nineteen of his first twenty albums had been number one in at least one of the major countries. And if anyone needed further proof of his popularity, Julio had awards from nearly every country and all the famous music industry publications.

Still, there were pockets of resistance to his charm and talents. While he could sell out the Florida Park, Madrid's best-known nightclub, and his record sales in Spain were respectable, he was not number one in his native land. And one of the most important Hispanic audiences, Mexico, also proved troublesome. Mexico was the link he sought to jump into the United States, and he persevered to break into it.

As 1972 drew to a close, Julio could look back with satisfaction and ahead with great expectations. In just four years he had won that long-sought goal—he was known as a troubadour to the world, a star on five continents. He was appreciative of his stardom but never self-centered enough to keep all the credit for himself. There were debts to be paid, and now was a good time to begin paying back for all his good fortune. Deep down, Julio felt a special obligation to his father. How could he repay the man who had been instrumental in all his successes, who had stood by him, encouraged him, and was still his main adviser? Dr. Iglesias did not need any money; he could provide handsomely for his family.

There was only one way Julio could thank his father—through his music, which, after all, can live on long after he is gone. Beautiful music, music that touches the hearts and souls of the people, survives death, disaster, and its own creators. In his effort to pay proper homage to his father, one of Julio's greatest songs was born. "Canto a Galicia" was recorded as a hymn to Dr. Iglesias' homeland, a song that throbbed with the emotions of Galicians throughout the world. And its success was not limited to Spain. The record swept through Latin America, Europe, North Africa, even the Middle East, where its haunting message was understood instantly by similarly displaced peoples. It became one of Julio's most requested concert numbers and the one he most often sang to close his show.

Despite the popularity of this song, Julio continued to be a bigger star outside Spain, which was undergoing social unrest. Franco was aging, and many were fearful about the country's political future after his death. Young Spaniards, the basic record buyers, were chafing under the dictatorship and were in sympathy with the youth movement sweeping the globe in the 1970s. Severely limited as they were by the Franco regime's attitude toward political expression, their only permissible means of protest was through their music and arts. Thus, the popular stars in Spain then were the protest singers, while the sweet romantic ballads of Julio Iglesias were ignored, except by the older women, who found solace in his voice.

Since he more than compensated for so-so sales in Spain with his performance everywhere else, CBS España continued with their promotion plans for him. After penetrating Japan and Germany, Julio was considered a highly salable commodity. As one Spanish CBS executive exclaimed, "Even without understanding what he means when he is singing, people all over Europe go crazy about Julio. We are going to record Julio in every possible language we can."

Julio, as of 1973, had ten million sold LPs to his credit and was stepping gingerly into the United States. His singles went gold, his albums platinum, and the Hispanic press hailed him as "The New Valentino." With the record royalties and concert profits rolling in, Julio also became one of the wealthiest men in Spain. Now instead of booking flights for his tours, Julio traveled in style, with his own jet to fly him from concert to concert. The rest was invested, principally in real estate. Wealthy Europeans believe in the value of land; Julio is no exception.

His real estate purchases served two purposes—they were wise investments and were in the sun belt, which gave Julio tanning spas of his own all over the world. Madrid, naturally, was his main residence, where his family lived. Next he bought a home in Mallorca (Majorca), one of Spain's most exclusive resorts, a ranch in Argentina, and a tropical paradise retreat in Tahiti. Thus, he would never have to suffer the rigors of winter.

Meanwhile, Isabel was often sitting at home while Julio

traipsed through the exciting foreign capitals. After Chaveli, she gave birth to their first son, Julio José, in 1973, and two years later to their last child, another boy, Enrique. To outsiders, it appeared to be a perfect family. While the children were young, they joined Julio in parts of his tours, but as they reached school age, that was difficult. There are celebrities who have sacrificed superstardom to preserve a stable family life, possibly because they disliked the constant travel. But while Julio valued home and hearth, his heart was on the road. He fully savored the material possessions his hard work brought him—the luxurious homes, the cars, the beautiful clothes, and the parties that introduced him to the VIPs of politics and business.

He especially valued talks with business leaders, as he had become a kind of one-man miniconglomerate. His tours were now major productions that returned many millions beyond the concert proceeds through the sales of what Brazilians call *griffe*. This is the merchandise that is sold before, during, and after concerts. Julio had a percentage of everything, from the records to the TV shows, his stardom generated—movies, T-shirts, even shorts, watches, and a line of cosmetics in South America. Whenever Julio appeared in person, sales leaped—another reason why he could not stop touring.

Julio Iglesias had, at thirty, finally reached the pinnacle of success. No one doubted that he was the world's number-one recording star. But if friends thought he would be satisfied, they were surprised. He sought new challenges; he had grown accustomed to the huge throngs of fans on the Hispanic circuit.

After breaking all previous records for performers, he now sought prestigious halls. In Germany he sang with the Berlin Philharmonic; in the United States he chose historic Carnegie Hall for his 1974 appearances. Both were well suited to his style of performing. Julio left the scruffy look to rock stars; his shows were the epitome of taste and elegance. He appeared in tuxedos throughout his performances—first in a custom-made black outfit, and after intermission in his custom-tailored white tux. This, he has always believed, sets the tone for his concerts, which are expertly mounted to enhance the romantic feeling of his love songs.

As early as 1976 Julio was discussing his plans to record an English-language album. But there were scoffers, critics who questioned his true popularity outside of the Hispanic zone. Perceptive ringsiders viewed him as less successful than his publicity hype claimed. In reviewing what his associates were hailing as a triumphant French performance, *Variety* noted that the Paris Olympic theater "audiences are well laced with members of the big population of Spanish expatriates living here." As for inspiring the French-born listeners, the reviewer added that "despite his easygoing style, he is obviously less in his element than back home and on the familiar Latin American circuit."

Julio has usually been supersensitive to any negative criticism, but he never retreats. Eventually he would win over the French and add the Italians to his victorious chain of countries. That left only the English-speaking regions, with the United States his ultimate goal.

Fortunately, Julio teamed with another rising Spanish songwriter, Ramón Arcusa, who was to become his closest friend and confidant, and his co-writer and record producer. They proved to be a winning combination; Julio is always quick to praise Arcusa and to attribute much of his success to Arcusa's musical talent.

So far he had confined his American tours to areas with large Latin concentrations; he was virtually unknown to the Anglo society. But CBS anticipated selling him to mainstream America, as long as Julio followed their advice.

There were drawbacks to this move. Non-English-speaking entertainers have never succeeded on a superstar level in America. Several Latin and Gallic celebrities had been promoted in years past, but aside from a fleeting sensation caused by Maurice Chevalier in the 1930s, most had been relegated to second billing—Xavier Cugat, Carmen Miranda, and, unless supported by his superstar wife Lucille Ball, Desi Arnaz, among others. Except for the British, Americans were not very receptive to foreign accents. Even supersexy Yves Montand had never been able to penetrate the American heartland with his French songs.

Julio was not blind to the obstacles, but he refused to be influenced by the failures of others. If there is one market that lures every success-oriented performer, it is the United States, where succeeding brings worldwide recognition and great wealth.

There may have been other, unspoken reasons leading Julio to the States, not the least of which was the changing political tide in Spain. Franco had handpicked his successor, but the country would no longer be controlled by a dictator. While Franco returned it to a monarchy, it was a constitutional one in which the ruler, King Juan Carlos, would be more figurehead than decision maker. Under the new king's sure hand, Spain held its first free elections in years and, as happens with repressed countries tasting freedom, the Spaniards gradually elected a socialist government. Such a government tends to make monied society nervous, although Spain has never resorted to appropriating property from the rich. But many wealthy people slip out of such places because the fear of this happening is always there. Whatever his motives, Julio added to his own real estate holdings with a house in Bel Air, California.

At the same time, CBS Records International took over his contract from their smaller Spanish subsidiary, preparatory to introducing Julio to the United States. "Naturally I'm nervous about the future," he told reporters about his next scheme, "but it's the opportunity of my life, and I don't intend to fail."

A major concert tour was planned that would take Julio to the Shrine Auditorium in Los Angeles and the cavernous Madison Square Garden in New York City, both in the heart of large Latin communities but with tremendous Anglo populations sophisticated enough to give some attention to a well-publicized foreign artist. Both concerts brought out the kind of crowds that encouraged CBS. At Madison Square Garden the singer shattered all past records for Latin entertainers by pulling in 70 percent capacity to that vast auditorium, a better sale than many American and English rock acts made there. Julio also met with satisfying enthusiasm from the music critics. One, who usually covered hard rock acts, even commented that it "was nice to hear one smooth voice fill this normally raucous hall." And there were no riots or crime incidents following Julio's show; it was a pleasurable experience from first song to last, one he also shared with the rest of his fans as it was beamed via satellite for a TV special to Latin America.

The Los Angeles concert was even more successful, much to the amazement of other Spanish performers. Until Julio appeared, the Hispanic audience had been fairly well shrugged off. Several prior Latin shows with as many as a dozen billed attractions had failed, whereas the Iglesias appearance drew overflow crowds at the Shrine. Perhaps it was due to Julio's masterful production or the fact that he "cast an elegant figure" in his black and his white tuxedos, or his flair for the dramatic. Whatever the reason, he had all the charisma necessary for superstardom.

The only dark note came from a Latin critic who carped that Julio's problem "is that if one looks beyond the style, beyond the glimmering shell, the aura and fascination simply evaporate. Taken for what he is, free of all hyped anticipation and regal trappings, Iglesias emerges as an above-average composer who is an uninspired performer and a mediocre singer."

But the final decision on Julio's success lay with the public. And they had their say the next day when happy record store owners reported that they had run out of Iglesias albums and were ordering more. With sales soaring, CBS International now had all the incentive they needed to go forward with their campaign for Julio to take on America. Knowledgeable insiders agreed that the company indeed had a hot property, and one very different from the current crop of superstars. Along with his talent for selling himself, Julio had a professional attitude the executives appreciated. During the last ten years they had had to cater to a rising tide of teenagers–turned overnight idols. Most were just like shooting stars—a streak on the charts, then instant oblivion. In between, however, totally ill-prepared for their sudden fame and riches, they were hell on wheels. Rock stars often were persona non grata at hotels where their kindred spirits had left lasting impressions of mischief and mayhem. Rockers also demanded exotic food, liquor, and perks for their friends, rarely thanking the help for their trouble. But the record labels and promoters were also to blame; as long as an act meant money in the bank, they were indulged and naturally came to believe in their own importance.

Julio was a welcome relief, a class act, totally professional. Through his business associates, he did demand a lot, but mainly in the way of lighting and equipment that made the Iglesias show more effective. And, of course, he was a tough negotiator in talking contracts and money, but he also delivered, even if it wound up costing him money to create a first-rate entertainment. But he had not gone into the business just for the money.

Behind this glamorous superstar is an ego he does his best to hide. With that Latin *chistoso* quality, he appears to deflect compliments from himself modestly, but he is always aware of the limelight and frequently on its edge. When he meets a reporter, he does not ask, "What is your name?" but inquires, "Whom do you work for?" And he is sensitive to how he is coming across in interviews, to the point that he seems to be manipulating the stories, deftly avoiding questions that get dangerously close to the parts of his life he wants to keep private. In public he always seems to be working, even at parties. And that may be the secret of his success. There are more talented artists, but no one can compare with Julio when it comes to promoting himself. Success, after all, is supposedly one-tenth talent and nine-tenths hard work and sweat.

Above all, though, once he chose pop music for his life's career, he never stopped studying the business. Driven by his healthy ego, he could never be satisfied to be just a popular star. Yet whenever his ambition is questioned, he shrugs off the implication that he works harder than most stars for his *número uno* status, explaining that he is "a working man, working at something I love very much." It is a love that has demanded many sacrifices on his part. He is a restless man who has spent most of his adulthood in recording studios, onstage, or rehearsing for both. When it comes to relaxing, he admits, "Maybe it's better to say I will take a vacation when I die."

That single-track mind works wonders for a career, but it wreaks havoc on a personal life. The day was coming when Julio would have to decide between that career and his wife. When it happened Julio was shocked; after he made his choice, he was shaken!

A Painful Parting

While Julio toured, his Latin lover reputation intact, Isabel was growing impatient in Madrid. Even though he called home every day, Isabel felt isolated with their three children. It was easy for Julio to proclaim, there "is no greater freedom than to be in love," because he was free to roam the world while she was tied down to a family. She was proud that he could fill Chile's national stadium in Santiago with one hundred thousand cheering fans for a concert, that his latest albums, *El Amor* and *33 Años*, soared to the top of the charts in Europe, Latin America, Canada, Africa, and the Middle East, but she needed more than her husband's publicity releases to make her home complete. They had more money than they could ever spend but no time together. It was similar to the story of Elvis and Priscilla Presley—and leading to the same sad end.

Isabel was giving the best years of her life to a man she almost never saw. His fans believed he was the luckiest guy in the world, but his private life was crumbling. When she asked for a divorce, it was not an easy decision. They had been married in a Catholic ceremony in an officially Catholic country; divorce seemed impossible, as Spain was still debating the question of granting civil divorces. But Isabel was firm in her resolve to make a new life for herself; she would find a way.

Julio, toiling happily in the playgrounds of the rich, was unaware of the drama about to unfold in his life. Certainly Isabel was welcome to join him, but she was not about to put her children in the care of nannies and servants. And Julio was unable to give up the road, so they were at an impasse.

The separation was handled very quietly. Neither wanted to be hounded by reporters or to have their problems aired in sensational newspapers. Their first consideration was for the children.

Isabel and Julio were still friends, though, which helped keep the parting amicable. No hint of scandal ever leaked out about their situation, but Julio's closest friends admitted he was very troubled when Isabel sought the divorce. Having his wife leave him so publicly was a jolt to his strong Latino macho feelings.

Fortunately, there was another upheaval taking place in his life that counterbalanced the divorce. One of the provisions of his new CBS International contract was an agreement that the singer would spend several months a year in the United States. Undoubtedly this was to allow CBS to promote him to American audiences with the assurance that he would be available to make appearances. Julio was happy to comply; it must have been a relief to move gracefully from Madrid with its memories of failed love, and he was glad CBS was targeting him to be their star of the 1980s.

Most record companies were facing the fact that many of their steady customers were a maturing audience, outgrowing rock with its new punk beat and New Wave bands. To keep them coming back to the racks, the labels needed to produce music to meet their changing life-styles. Romantic singers had been out since the late 1950s, but music, they knew, ran in cycles, and the pendulum could be swung back to softer, more melodic tunes, the exact type of love songs that were the Iglesias specialty.

Julio was attractive to the woman over twenty-five with strong romantic urges, the type of woman who buys gothic and romance novels. And as a single, available man, one who had lost at love, his vulnerability was all the more appealing. A new sadness tinged his love songs, and Julio basked in his female fans' sympathy, sighing, "If I had been successful in love, I wouldn't be able to sing as I do."

He also discovered advantages to being a bachelor again. Seeking events that would give him broad exposure on American television, Julio was pleased to be asked to judge the 1979 Miss Universe contest. As an added plus, it was taking place in Australia, where he confessed he was struck by the beauty of the women—and the beaches.

However, this kind of publicity can backfire in the age of modern, liberated women, so to curb any possible criticism from anti–beauty contest factions, Julio explained that he, too, had doubts about their meaningfulness. Admitting, "I love beautiful women," he added that he didn't "much care for beauty contests. I sometimes think of them as cattle fairs." But he never turned down the invitations to judge them.

Meanwhile, sales of his single "Emociones" were soaring, and CBS urged him to put his efforts into learning English and recording his first American LP. The reception and reviews he was getting for his concerts in America's Hispanic areas were encouraging, but Julio also knew that the company was hedging its bets on his future success.

CBS, of course, is in business to make money. And there are no guarantees that any one act will fulfill the promise that even the most astute talent promoter sees in an artist. Too many fortunes have been spent on "sure things" in the record business for any company to get overconfident about its picks for stardom. What CBS was banking on was being in the right place at the right time with the right new sound, in this case Latin, when the fickle public was looking for something different. The Latin beat had swept much of the world; it was logical to believe that America would be no exception.

But Julio Iglesias was not the only star they were launching with the Latin beat; he was just one of a series of Hispanic hit-makers they were introducing on this side of the Atlantic. Ultimately, the one who succeeded would be the one with the greatest drive, willing to make the most sacrifices: Julio Iglesias.

He was the one willing to take the risks, to experiment and reach beyond the safe Hispanic audiences. Taking that path made all the difference. As he played to bigger U.S. audiences, he caught the attention of the mainstream press. A reviewer for England's biggest pop rock paper, *Melody Maker,* was sufficiently impressed at a New York Iglesias concert that his commentary was run in the paper, even though Julio's was not the kind of act normally reviewed therein. But, with a change in the air, *Melody Maker* sang his praises, noting that he "is just what you'd expect from an Iberian crooner, clear, soulful vibrato indulgently melodic on choruses and gently syncopated on verses . . . a proper song-seller." By way of explanation for this deviation from their usual rock act review, the writer added, "Iglesias is one of the earth's biggest stars, having sold over 20 million albums. The past year *A Mis 33 Años* and *Emociones* have won 28 gold records between them, including 6 platinums."

Clearly the CBS influence was taking hold, with such non-Latin critics now invited to attend Julio's concerts and to talk to him. Gracious as ever, Julio discussed his career with reporters at every opportunity, but now instead of filling their notebooks with quotes about his worldwide successes, he concentrated on selling himself as part of the American market as well.

People wondered why he would risk his position as the world's premier recording star by putting his reputation on the line in the United States, which had never been hospitable to non-English-speaking foreigners.

It was difficult for Julio to put his reasons into words. What made the United States so alluring was the terrible risk, the possibility of failure, a danger Julio had not experienced in years and a challenge he missed. Merely repeating his past successes was boring.

Yes, he conceded, there was always the hidden possibility of rejection once he undertook this new adventure. But he went into the project confident of victory. Besides, he said, "I'm a fighter. I have money to buy the companies I am working for. But I start to fight again like a young artist. . . . I don't have time to spend my money and still I want to fight with this country. . . . It is a big country, and it's a difficult one. It's like David fighting Goliath. But I have to do it."

It was a battle he had been preparing for during the past years. And now that the moment was at hand, he claimed, "I'm psychologically prepared for whatever's going to happen in my incursion into the American market." It wasn't, after all, as if he were a novice. "I'm a disciplined and creative professional," he reminded his inquisitors. What it boiled down to was a purely personal ambition, or as he insisted, "In show business this is *the* country and . . . all the European artists, we try to do something in this country. . . . It's partly ego, vanity, many things together."

The campaign began in earnest in 1979, after his marital separation, when he took up residence in Los Angeles. CBS cranked up their skillful publicity department to hype Julio Iglesias as the Spanish Sinatra and the New Valentino. The publicity began paying off when he returned to play Madison Square Garden again. One ringsider remarked that "the ladies in the house . . . swooned, whistled, made suggestive gestures, blew kisses, and threw roses at their idol." The enthusiasm with which his performance was received was likened to the kind of reception usually reserved for Tom Jones, reaffirming the record company's faith in Julio's chances of crossing over to the U.S. market. One CBS insider proclaimed Julio "the most universal singer in the Hispanic world, and because the creative vacuum in the U.S. favors the possible appearance of a Latin singer, CBS [would] launch him in the American market with songs, music, and arrangements suitable for the market."

What they overlooked in their plans in 1979 were Julio's exceptionally high standards. It was CBS's plan to rush him onto the U.S. scene with whatever material he could record immediately. But while the Spanish Sinatra was just as anxious to make a big splash in the States, he could not forsake his perfectionism.

It is not unusual for Julio to spend as much as a year refining an album of his songs. He seems to have a sixth sense about his music, a feel for just what works and what doesn't. Often that has made the difference between respectable sales and enormous ones. It happened, he remembers, when he was expected to deliver his album *Hey.* To everyone else, the LP was ready to be pressed and shipped, but Julio stepped forward to say, "No! This isn't right." He could not put his objection into words; it was something he heard that only his musical sense could comprehend. He spent another three months on the project and was proved right when the album became one of his hottest hits. "In just a few seconds you put together the work of a lifetime," he explains. And he adds, "That's very exciting."

Between moving to California, concentrating on learning English, and producing an American record, Julio was able to work his way through the tragedy of losing Isabel. She, in the meantime, had been investigating the possibility of getting an annulment, which would permit her to remarry in the Catholic faith. Obtaining that piece of paper in Roman Catholic countries was harder than striking gold. Even civil divorce was outlawed in Spain at the time.

Cynics have long contended that for the rich anything is possible, even annulments in the Catholic Church. Technically, the annulment can be granted by any diocese, so through the years certain dioceses had gained a reputation for leniency in this area. Such dioceses were in countries without any official religion, countries that supported all the major beliefs.

The nation best fitting this description, of course, is the United States. And New York City's Brooklyn diocese was then granting more annulments than most other countries put together. In certain circles the diocese was even referred to as an annulment mill, a district where the wealthy and famous were always welcome, although many poor and middle-class Americans also were granted annulments there.

Annulment proceedings, whether in New York City or Rome, are, naturally, private matters. But in Brooklyn the grounds for annulment most frequently accepted as just cause was "severe psychological immaturity." This would cover couples who had children and therefore could not ask for an annulment on the other main ground: nonconsummation of the marriage. In such countries as Spain and Italy annulments were not granted on the ground of "severe psychological immaturity."

In 1979 Isabel, accompanied by her good friend the Duquesa de Cádiz, Franco's granddaughter, flew into New York to testify and pick up the papers for both a divorce and the annulment. Isabel received a generous settlement, and Julio was to have unlimited visiting rights with his children.

To this day Isabel is one of his dearest and closest friends. Nobody can ever be mad at Julio, especially not Isabel.

With his marriage officially finished, Julio concentrated solely on his career. While he kept insisting, "I want my woman to be my woman, to share everything with me and be together," the truth is, Julio cannot share his career. And since that career was his mistress and had already cost him one wife, he was beginning to doubt the wisdom of marrying again.

And yet losing Isabel had left a void in his life and an ache in his heart. But the void and the ache, he knew, could be healed by his fans. As long as he continued to devote long hours to pleasing them, the spotlight would never dim for him. He might not be able to hold on to one woman—but he could hold on to the millions who knew him only from his records and concerts and were devoted to him.

In the years after Isabel he has surrounded himself with beautiful women, some more meaningful to him than others. But whenever he is asked about a new relationship, the marriage-shy superstar calmly explains that Isabel "filled my life for the largest period of time, she's given me three children, and so far she is the most significant history, the most complete." He leaves the clear implication that once was enough for him on the marriage-go-round.

Isabel, however, liked the idea of marriage. After their divorce she began dating, and less than two years after leaving Julio, she fell in love with a handsome Spanish nobleman, Carlos Filco, the Marqués de Grounnon.

The Marqués is from one of Spain's finest old families. For many generations they have been settled on a lovely estate, which includes a vineyard, a winery, and other farm acreage. It was there, in a small, old-fashioned church maintained on the estate grounds, that Isabel, wearing a beautiful pink dress, married for the second time.

Since then the couple have become the adoring parents

of their own baby, a daughter they named Tamara. Julio's children love their baby half sister very much, and because Isabel encourages this close family feeling, she has allowed Tamara to travel with the older children when they visit Julio. Julio fell in love with the new baby, too, and he acts like a doting parent toward her, sending her toys from wherever he travels.

Julio is glad that Isabel has found peace and happiness with Carlos Filco. But even with this happy example before him, he himself is not going to rush into a second marriage.

·5·

Parties and Playgirls

*A*s he settled into Los Angeles to forget his personal problems, Julio felt there was still something wrong. Usually he had no trouble adjusting to any new environment. Certainly there was nothing wrong with the climate; it was warm and sunny. His rented house was airy and spacious. The people were friendly and gracious, and yet something was missing.

Then he realized the reason: in Los Angeles he was considered a wealthy, handsome hunk—but not a superstar. It did not matter in the least to the entertainment giants that he was the number-one recording artist in the world; he was a complete unknown in the United States—where it counted with them. Because of their screen and record triumphs most of them were recognized anywhere in the world; only Julio could walk down Rodeo Drive unnoticed.

No one was rude; he was invited to all the right parties, but more for his money and smooth manners, which made him a sought-after extra man, than for his talent. To a man who unashamedly confesses, "I love my picture on the front page. I don't like the inside ones," obscurity was a humbling, unsatisfying experience. If you "are not successful yet," he says, don't live in Los Angeles, because it is "very sad out there."

Before he could get too depressed, CBS International and his business representatives worked out a new movie to star Julio, with his label simultaneously releasing the sound-track album. It also helped him to make the psychological break from Isabel. *Todos los Días, Un Día (All the Days, One Day)* was very autobiographical. Julio played himself in this slight story about the loneliness of endless travel from city to city. It tells of his taking a break between his Paris and New York concert dates to stop in Panama to romp in the sun. In that Pacific paradise he meets a tall, willowy blond archaeology student to whom his show business world is absolutely alien. Her youth, beauty, and innocence rejuvenate Julio, and in their time together she sees some of the sadness that follows entertainment idols. A couple of American stars—Carol Lynley and Tony Martin—had small parts but were not enough to interest U.S. theaters in playing it. Back in Los Angeles, Julio was still unrecognized.

But with so much of show business centered out there, he might still be a Californian if not for the fact that his record label, CBS International, was based in Miami. CBS, Inc., the parent corporation, makes its headquarters in New York, which has the most thriving recording studios. But the smaller subsidiary caters to the Hispanic market, and Miami has become the gateway linking the U.S.A. to Latin America. Julio went to Miami and instantly felt at home.

Miami has a strong Latin flavor that reminded him of home. In Los Angeles the Spanish community consists mainly of Mexicans, and their neighborhoods are worlds apart from the fancy residences of Beverly Hills and Bel Air, where Julio resided. The two societies never meet, whereas in Miami, although it also is segregated into economic zones of poor, middle-class, and wealthy, they all mingle throughout the city.

Hispanic immigrants overwhelmed the American population in Miami during the last decade as they pushed their way in from Central and South America. Cubans, Colombians, Spaniards, Argentinians, Salvadorans—immigrants or refugees from every country south of the U.S. border, the people who had always embraced Julio, who infused him with their joy and enthusiasm—were all there, with his favorite foods, music, and life-style.

It did not take him long to pack up and move to Miami. Surrounded by his compatriots once more, Julio felt right at home and missed his beloved Spain less. And the Latinos were honored to have a superstar they equated with Sinatra or Burt Reynolds so close. The flourishing Spanish press in Miami was also delighted because just as American superstars' exploits sell papers, Julio's moves do the same for Latin tabloids.

The first order of business was to find a home that would meet all his standards. He was directed to an exclusive, secluded island just off Miami called Indian Creek, an island paradise just minutes away from the bustling center of Miami. Julio loved it at first sight. Here he could lie for hours on his own private white beaches, away from prying eyes.

Connected to the mainland by a lantern-lighted bridge, the estate has a main house with three spacious bedrooms, a huge living room, a kitchen, a breakfast room, a media room, and lots of open space. Completely enclosed by a security gate manned by twenty-four-hour guards, the hideaway is reached by crossing the bridge, then driving along bay roads and up a long circular driveway leading to the mansion that is set well back on the palm-tree-lined estate's extensive acreage. Visitors can admire the lush green lawns, perfectly trimmed, before entering the front door. Once inside, guests pass along a marble hallway that doubles as a landscaped atrium, winding up in the living room.

Perhaps the feature that sold Julio on the property was

the three swimming pools, including one inside the house. The spectacular estate enchanted Julio. He didn't even blink when he heard the price—three million dollars. It would be the perfect diversion to help him relax while he plunged into the scary new territory of the United States. He allows few hobbies to distract him from his studio sessions, but he has always been interested in architecture and decorating. Redoing this mansion would surely engross him.

Revitalized by the challenge, he decided to give the place a "Mediterranean look," one full of light and air. The enormous living room presented the most trouble. Large picture windows offer wonderful views of the bay and are restful to the eye, but during the day the sultry midday Miami sun is too strong even for an enthusiast like Julio. He wanted to be able to control light in the room without losing the airiness.

It was a costly choice. Julio, the perfectionist, was not happy with the room after its first redecorating, and a second left him still dissatisfied. Since he spends so much time in the house, he hired a third set of decorating experts to produce what he had in mind. This time he relied on his two favorite decorators, Jaime Parlade, from Marbella, Spain, and Mario Connio, a Madrid-based Argentinian architect-designer. They followed Julio's specific instructions that the room must have such a relaxed atmosphere that he "could fall asleep anywhere" in it.

The results elated the singer. Plush, dreamy powder-blue couches dominate the room, and overstuffed, soft pillows are scattered all over the deep beige carpets. Expensive Italian pink onyx marble tables add a splash of color. In the morning the windows are open to the stunning view of the water and Julio's forty-foot boat tied up at the pink dock. Later the teak blinds are drawn to filter out the harsh rays of the sun. By night those same blinds create a peaceful scene hand-painted by noted artist Tim Behrens for a mural effect.

There is an ample pool house by the larger outdoor swimming pool. Visitors relaxing on the chaise lounges beside the pool are usually awed by the combination of simplicity and formality of the Iglesias home. The home has a casual atmosphere, but guests are served, even outdoors, by white-gloved butlers.

To maintain the estate properly, Julio requires a full staff of cooks, gardeners, chauffeurs, along with Julio's private secretary, an old school chum from Madrid. And the staff and co-workers from his office can also be found running in and out all day. Despite the many servants, the home atmosphere is warm and inviting, never stuffy; it merely reflects the gracefully elegant manner of its owner. After his expensive Eden was finally finished, he sighed, "I love the peace here. The ocean is very calm."

Those who have known Julio for many years, however, can sense a touch of melancholy permeating the atmosphere. Pictures of his three children are scattered throughout the rooms, and one feels his loss, although the children visit him frequently. For the first few years in Miami his mother shared his house, having informally separated from Dr. Iglesias. His father remained in Madrid, where he still had an active medical practice, but he flew to Miami every few weeks to stay in touch with his sons.

As Julio's star was rising and his financial dealings were becoming complex, he persuaded his brother, Carlos, to leave his surgical practice in Madrid and take over the running of Julio's personal fortune. With his growing entourage and worldwide travels, Julio needed someone he considered absolutely trustworthy to handle his business. That meant Carlos, and when Julio's affairs shifted to Miami, Carlos and his family moved to a home nearby. They are a close family, sharing everything, and to Julio, Carlos' emotional support was as important as his financial acumen.

Julio needs to have his loved ones around him. He is very sensitive, very emotional, with a temper that can explode one minute and be all smiles the next. His energy level is high, so he constantly seeks outlets to ease his restlessness. Redesigning his house had served such a purpose, but finally the work was completed. Once the decorating of the home was completed, right down to the expensive abstract paintings by Hispanic artists on the walls, Julio seemed a bit sad—the same feeling he gets whenever a record, after much striving for perfection, has been finished.

While he views his palatial estate with satisfaction nowadays, he sometimes wishes he had it to do over again. "When I was renovating this house, I was engrossed in the work and very happy," he says. He had worked like an artist with an empty canvas, filling in his basic outline with various vital shadings. "Each day I would plan a room, the windows, or the exterior," he recalls. "But once this house was redone, I suddenly got very depressed. And now I know why. It was simply that everything had been finished. What makes my life meaningful is the feeling that I'm active, doing something, that I'm being challenged and my work is never complete."

He takes the same discipline into the recording studio. He trains like a fighter to keep in shape for his rigorous concert and studio schedule. There is little wasted motion in his days, although anyone watching him would at first envy him his daily routine.

When he is in Miami, the routine rarely varies. A night person, Julio usually sleeps until ten or eleven in the morning. He casually leafs through the newspaper over coffee in his breakfast nook, then disappears into the living room or bedroom to phone pals around the world for the latest gossip. Julio loves the hour or two of gossip best of all, and his friends know he is a good listener and adviser.

After that, Julio puts in at least two hours of physical exercise in his private gym, usually floor exercises to help him maintain his smooth rhythm and breath control. Then he takes a dip in the pool. He realizes how much his career depends on his lithe, athletic appearance, and he is proud of having maintained the same weight—165 pounds—on his nearly six-foot frame for the last twenty years. And he is quick to admit it is because "I exercise so my tummy is always the same." The payoff comes onstage when female fans audibly sigh over the handsome figure he cuts in his perfectly tailored tuxedos. He not only sounds like every woman's dream lover; he looks the part.

After a few laps in the pool he suns a bit to keep his tan healthy, then takes a run on the lawns with his two longtime companions, his dogs, Hey, a large pointer named for his platinum LP, whom Julio laughingly calls the king of the house, and Nathalie, the younger pointer.

By then he is ready to do a little business. For the most part he leaves the daily financial planning to Carlos, but he is involved with the concert schedules and record releases. Since he performs in so many countries, each with complex monetary policies and tax situations, he is thankful Carlos is willing to oversee this time-consuming part of his career. Julio rarely visits the Biscayne Boulevard offices that maintain his many enterprises. He prefers to spend time singing and composing at the white grand piano in his living room.

After a late lunch, a nap, and a shower, by five in the afternoon, just when most people are heading home from work, Julio's real day begins as he drives to the recording studios. He is fortunate that Miami offers highly sophisticated, state-of-the-art studio facilities, thanks largely to the Bee Gees, who are among the first successful U.S.-based superstars to discover the benefits of Miami. Barry,

Maurice, and Robin Gibb made Miami the base of their operations in the 1970s, and as they are also all successful producers, they made it fashionable for other stars to fly down for sessions.

Even without the professional-quality studios, Julio would have settled in Miami because of the people and he Spanish ambiance. But since his work takes precedence over everything else, he believes he has been extraordinarily lucky.

Julio doesn't really come alive until he steps inside a studio. This is where he really spends his life, recording, rerecording, mixing and remixing until that certain something clicks in his head and he knows that glossy Julio Iglesias sound has been achieved. Nothing is ever released outside those walls until he is satisfied.

Many recording stars take a year or more to produce their albums, but more often than not the records are put together at random moments during that year, between concerts and playtime. And many of them will settle for filler cuts, songs to stretch the platter to an acceptable length, songs that could not be released as singles. Julio disdains such practices.

The way he sees it, too many "artists don't represent what they sing. I really sing what I represent so the lyrics and the music seem to match." That "match" can take upward of nine months of intensive ten-hour days to accomplish. Even on tour, if he has a free day, he often will book time at a local studio to work on an album. And since he has released as many as eight albums a year, each one personalized to an individual country for local sales, he is often under tremendous pressure.

His day ends about 3 A.M. when he returns home to his favorite meal, a seafood dinner, supervised by his mother when she is in residence. This routine is varied only when he is touring, and even then not by much. The time he spends at home in the studio is used to rehearse and refine his act. Beyond that, much of his time is spent at publicity affairs and private parties where his presence puts him in touch with important people and contacts.

Somewhere in between, CBS urged him to study English more intensively because the company was eager to get him launched. Julio, too, wanted to get on with his first U.S. album and was talking to Barry Gibb about producing it. Ramón Arcusa, his gifted, longtime co-writer and producer, would also be in the studio, but both believed that because of the peculiarities of the American market, Julio needed the guidance of a knowledgeable music man who had a string of successful U.S. albums to his credit. Gibb was perhaps the hottest pop producer around. Besides his own Bee Gees *Saturday Night Fever* disc, which up to that point was the most successful LP of all time, Gibb had spun out number-one albums for Barbra Streisand and Dionne Warwick. Gibb and Iglesias were a natural combination also because both were expatriates from Europe.

But the LP was put on hold because Julio had to keep touring if he was to continue his expensive life-style. There was another Miss Universe contest to judge, and since it took place in New York, he agreed to participate again. While he was still not heard of in the American tabloids, his Hispanic fans were vitally interested in his every word, thought, and deed in the United States, and copies of his records practically flew out of the stores.

Now Julio conquered the heart of yet another country, Israel. That beleaguered Middle East nation was undergoing an undeniable renaissance of Spanish music in the early 1980s. One observer close to the Israeli pop scene credited the skyrocketing popularity of Spanish love songs to the fact that the people were "looking for tender, comforting, romantic songs to take them away from the pressures of the present." Israel, torn by wars and internal strife, found the

Spanish songs soothing because, it was often noted, the sounds were similar to Hebrew. One important Israeli disc jockey prophesied that Julio's music would soon be tops in popularity, recalling that in "the 1960s, it was Italian music. In the late 1970s, it was Brazilian. In the 1980s, it will be Spanish songs, of everyday life and unhappy love affairs, sort of Spanish country and western." And Julio, already a chart buster in Israel, easily won the people by adding a few songs in Hebrew to his repertoire.

Israel had other charms for Julio—beautiful women. It was while touring the Middle East that Julio met the first woman to captivate him since Isabel. Mutual friends introduced them, and Julio was immediately struck by Sydne Rome's blonde beauty. An actress, Sydne was appearing in several European movies and was being groomed for stardom. Graceful, slim, she was Julio's ideal of a woman, and friendship blossomed into romance.

Sydne was different from most of the women Julio had known; she was career-minded and not about to depend on a man to make her happy. He was not used to an independent type, but he thought this trait endearing—for a time. Their careers often separated them, but to Sydne it was a serious affair. Julio did not know how serious until Sydne risked her life to be near him. On a day of heavy bombing he was startled to find she had "crossed Lebanon from Beirut to the ruins where the sun never sets, in a truck, dressed as a mechanic, just to be with me for a few hours."

But she soon learned that Julio is more of a flirt than a constant lover. While he often sighs that he is "someone who is waiting for love, and I know that someplace someone is waiting too," he seems more in love with the idea of romance than with the real thing.

When they parted, it was obvious that she regretted having been involved with such a playboy. Her frank comments on her experience with Julio indicated that he definitely was not on her list of favorite people. When questioned about the possibility of their patching things up, she shot back with: "If he got down on his knees, I still wouldn't go back to him."

Apparently the problem was that she learned he was flirting with other women behind her back, and that was too much. "If I wanted, I could destroy Julio Iglesias," she told one reporter. Sydne freely admitted that she "fell in love with his elegance and his style of life that surrounds him. Julio is elegance, his cars, his houses, his clothes . . . even his underwear." But, she added, it finally got to be too much. "I got tired. I said, 'Enough.' Besides," she added with perhaps a touch of malice, "I realized he was aging, and I don't like old men."

If Julio was hurt by that low blow, he was too gentlemanly to fall to Sydne's level. After all, when it comes to fidelity, he says, "I have more constant preoccupations." Running free as he now was in such bachelors' paradises as Paris, Monte Carlo, Hollywood, and New York, Julio considered women merely diversions from his career. Many could know him; none could hold him.

Julio put the Rome affair behind him with little trouble. His schedule was full; he sang in Egypt at their pyramids at the request of President and Mrs. Anwar Sadat, who had become close personal friends. Princess Grace of Monaco, ever his champion, invited him to participate in her famous Red Cross Ball at the palace in Monaco. His talent, poise, and cultured manner was opening doors at the highest level of society. Many blue bloods and jet setters proudly displayed complete sets of his albums, and they were the first to buy tickets to his concerts.

Julio never disappointed them. Other acts have their good and bad nights, but Julio has never given an inferior performance. The same time-consuming effort he gives to perfecting his discs, he also devotes to his stage appearances. Onstage, the concert seems to be tossed off casually, but each movement has been carefully synchronized with the music; nothing is left to chance in an Iglesias show. Not only does he have the music and moves down pat; whenever he introduces new material, he listens and studies audience reaction until he has smoothed the latest number to blend with the rest of the act. He considers himself a consummate professional, an artist who can send fans into a frenzy with the slightest vocal inflection and a minimum of suggestive stage movement.

From the first moment he stepped on a stage, Julio never doubted his ability to sell himself to his own people. His romantic ballads have the same effect on Hispanics as country and western ballads do on Southerners and Southwesterners in the U.S.

The gracefully choreographed Julio Iglesias spectacular in concert is the result of Julio's high regard for his fans. They have chosen him to be a superstar, and he feels a responsibility to fulfill their expectations. The responsibility weighs heavily on him. He says candidly that to "the Spanish-speaking world, as a singer, I am a leader. They are waiting for something musical, and my lyrics are stories that are very simple, common, and even naïve. . . . It's musical talk. Not sophisticated or intellectual chatter. I think I represent the little stories between couples in the world. That is, perhaps, my success in my own language— capturing the little histories."

Critics, even those who have reservations about his vocal quality, have lauded him for his showmanship. In a creative vacuum in which millionaire musicians are no-shows or are jumping all over the stage in torn sweat shirts, sneakers, and tight jeans while shrieking unintelligible sounds into over-amped microphones, which is what U.S. youths, who comprise the majority of ticket buyers, demand, Julio is a welcome relief. He is a throwback to the crooners of the

1940s and 1950s who could be distinguised by their strongly individual styles. One reviewer summed Julio up best when he exclaimed, "Where too many MOR [middle of the road] artists are affected by the shabbiness of a tired show business esthetic, Julio Iglesias projects the kind of ease that hasn't been seen since the days of the black-tied big band crooner."

And it is an act that is returning many of the forgotten music fans to concert halls. Through him, the older generations are rediscovering popular music, and even when the language is foreign, Julio gets the message across. As a hard-working artist, he believes that in music "what is important is the feeling. If I have that, then people understand even in countries where they don't know my words."

But he knew that to reach mainstream Americans, he would have to deliver songs they understood, in their own language. Throughout his yearly tours of Egypt, Israel, Australia, Europe, and South America, he traveled with an English tutor, still determined by the end of the year to begin his overdue United States record. And he continued to make new conquests of women. Performing in Virginia at a benefit for the famed Wolf Trap Theater, he enthralled President Ronald Reagan's wife, Nancy, who promised him an invitation to sing at the White House.

His own love life was also on the upswing when he began dating Virginia Sipi, a stunning blonde model. The curvaceous Caracas, Venezuela, native became his favorite companion, between her own modeling assignments. She brought a new spring to Julio's step and a new lilt to his voice whenever he talked about her.

The courtship heated up so intensely that even friends who knew of his strong aversion to marriage began to wonder if Virginia might not get him to the altar again. Julio could not stop rhapsodizing about Virginia, claiming she "made me happy, intensely happy in a very short time."

Usually Julio is reticent about his personal life. When he is asked about his career, he can go on for hours, with the minutest details about his past, present, and future plans. But he clams up when the conversation swings around to questions about himself or his family. It is almost as if he were hiding a deep, dark secret about his past, but he really just dislikes putting his loved ones through the publicity mill.

It was surprising, then, when he was so open about his romance with Virginia. But he also seemed to be setting himself up for rejection when he revealed he thought she was "splendid, young and burning her precious youth by my side, always going from here to there." Almost in disbelief he added that Virginia even "waits for me to awake."

Julio's exuberance was catching. Virginia got caught up in it. Believing they had a true commitment, she openly professed her love for him. "I adore him," she bubbled, adding, "Sure we're going to get married." As to when, she hinted mysteriously that the two would "soon have a surprise."

When that "surprise" failed to materialize, Virginia stood right by her man, never letting on if she felt hurt, implying there were private reasons for the delay. "I can't force Julio to publicly announce that I am the woman in his life," she explained. "I love him and I know he loves me. I am important to him. He has his reasons [for not announcing their engagement], and if they're his, then there's no reason why they should be revealed."

This naturally had the press and fans confused. Was he or wasn't he getting married? When Julio heard of the controversy, he nearly exploded. To a writer trying to pin him down on the subject, he said, "I am not getting married. No way! Are you crazy?"

Virginia got the point. Their romance trailed off, although they are still good friends and even date occasionally. But now Virginia no longer has stars in her eyes—at least not for this song star. She realizes that Julio wants to remain free.

There were moments, no doubt, when Julio missed the closeness he'd had with Isabel, but there were consolations. Mainly, his family, who brought him great happiness. They were never far from his thoughts. But just ahead, as 1981 drew to a close, were danger and fear. Julio was on an unbelievable roll of good luck; every year he topped his record in sales and concert audiences; he was pampered, showered with love, once again one of life's fair-haired boys. It was all similar to his youth, when the sun seemed never to stop shining on him, lighting up each day with a special glow just for the Iglesias clan. Back then tragedy had struck just as Julio had his first dream within his reach. And he had survived, but not without pain.

Now he was about to learn that there is always a price to be paid for success, only this time the fear and pain would strike someone he held dearer than himself. It would be a shocking blow, all the more frustrating because he would not be able to take any action. There would be nothing to do but wait—and pray. And just as the car crash had left permanent scars on both his body and psyche, so would this new tragedy.

·6·

The Kidnapping

*D*r. Iglesias always celebrated Christmas with his family, even after he separated from his wife. He also enjoyed traveling with Julio whenever his schedule permitted, so it was not unusual for him to accompany his son on his successful tour of Argentina in 1981. It was a special treat for Julio whenever his father could join him; they have a very close, special relationship. In fact, he unabashedly confesses, "I always preferred my father. . . . My father is part of me. He is my soul. Today like tomorrow."

After the tour, father and son returned to Julio's home for the holidays. In typical Iglesias style, the house was full of laughter and warmth, even though no one outside the family's small circle of intimate friends was allowed to intrude.

Due to his busy practice at several Madrid clinics, Dr. Iglesias had to fly back home before New Year's. Julio went to the airport to see him off, setting off a chain of events that would leave the entire family near collapse.

The doctor arrived home safely, but not long after that he disappeared. Julio's father was an important man in Spain, and not just because of his son's fame. Yet it was Julio's fame that put the doctor's life in danger.

It did not take long for word to leak out that Julio's father was missing. And because information was not readily available, it did not take long for conflicting reports to confuse the situation. In the Iglesias case the news media rushed out headlines without having all the correct facts.

Several people gave what each swore was an eyewitness report about Dr. Iglesias' movements on December 29, the day he disappeared. One paper reported the doctor had arrived at a Madrid clinic that morning as expected, parked his car, was seen entering a travel agency with two men, and had not been heard from thereafter. The janitor of another clinic testified to seeing the doctor nearby with two young men, one of whom appeared to be holding a weapon under his coat. According to the janitor, Dr. Iglesias left his own car parked at the clinic and went off with the men. Still another witness had the doctor being taken from his home by several men who had identified themselves as employees of a foreign television company there to interview him about Julio.

One report said the doctor disappeared at midday after working at the Provincial Institute of Gynecology and Obstetrics, and another claimed it was while he was on duty at the O'Donnell Clinic. It was a very confusing time. The only common element in all the stories was the fact that Julio's father was missing. As it turned out, most of the early reports had at least a few of their facts straight, but the whole story did not come out until Dr. Iglesias was freed after a harrowing three weeks.

Since violence had not been used in the abduction, no one had cause to worry about Dr. Iglesias until he failed to turn up for a 3 P.M. luncheon date on December 29. Even that, while out of character for a man as meticulous as the doctor, was not enough to arouse suspicion. But when he missed a clinic appointment later that afternoon, questions were asked.

Concerned friends called Dr. Iglesias' attorney. When his quiet investigation failed to turn up any evidence of his client's whereabouts, he phoned the police. With no information to go on except the fact that Dr. Iglesias had not been seen for several hours, the police treated it as a missing person case.

But as they started investigating, the reports from witnesses were disturbing. They had to suspect the worst, that Dr. Iglesias, a prominent and wealthy citizen, had been kidnapped.

In this type of situation, the police usually put a clamp on any kind of publicity, for fear the kidnappers will get scared and harm their victim. Thus the conflicting accounts in the papers were basically the result of various reporters' legwork. When the true facts were sifted out of all the stories, a scenario was pieced together that indicated Dr. Iglesias had indeed left a clinic and been accosted by two men who introduced themselves as German TV technicians. Dr. Iglesias was not suspicious because he had been contacted before by their colleagues. Their story was that they wanted to do a feature on Julio and needed an interview from his father. The doctor, always willing to cooperate to further Julio's career, unwittingly played into his abductors' hands.

First reports were still sketchy, but the family lawyer realized that Julio and the others would have to be notified in Miami. Since Carlos handled most of the family's business, the attorney contacted him. Carlos then had to decide how to break the news to Julio before he heard it on the radio or someone called the house. Julio was the sensitive one in the family, the one who could be emotionally shattered by such news, especially as the bond between father and son was so strong. As a doctor, Carlos was prepared to give what medical assistance he could to Julio, but he could not bear to go to Julio and break the devastating news to him.

Carlos placed a call to Isabel, who was vacationing in Switzerland. No one at this early stage could tell if other members of the Iglesias family were also in danger, but Carlos was taking no chances. The news was a shock, and because she is still very close to Julio, Isabel, too, was concerned about what effect the tragedy would have on him. Perhaps it was best that she be the one to break it to Julio.

When Isabel and Carlos were through talking, she put through her own call to Julio. Just as everyone expected, the singer was in a state of near collapse when he heard the news. One insider at the Indian Creek mansion reported that after Julio put the phone down, he "lay shaken on a sofa."

It did not take long for the kidnapping to hit the news wire services, and the story made headlines around the world. Reporters flocked to the Indian Creek estate, but they were disappointed by the lack of information coming from the house. Julio and his family were under strict orders from the Spanish police not to say anything to the media, as it could put his father in further jeopardy.

In Spain, however, rumors were rampant that the authorities suspected there were political motives behind the kidnapping. While it was true the doctor did not engage in any noticeable political activities, he was regarded as a staunch conservative. Perhaps it was just a bonus that his son was an international superstar, certainly rich enough to meet any ransom demands, and famous enough to provide the activist group responsible with more media coverage than they'd get from snatching the relative of an ordinary millionaire.

Whatever the police privately thought, they put a tight lid on their own actions to save Dr. Iglesias. They realized the crime was receiving worldwide attention, and they were not about to do anything rash while the spotlight was on them.

If Dr. Iglesias was harmed, they would be subjected to harsh criticism; their only objective was to get him back in one piece, and as soon as possible. If they could rescue him safely and quickly, it would reflect well on them in the world community.

Meanwhile, the family was mobilizing in Miami. Carlos went to Miami's International Airport and took the first available flight to Madrid to represent the Iglesiases on the scene. Julio's manager, Alfredo Fraile, stated that the superstar "won't move from here. If it is a kidnapping, they will try to contact him here in Miami."

The most immediate action, however, was to increase the security force at the estate. The New Year's Eve party scheduled for Carlos' home two nights later was hastily canceled; Julio arranged with Barry Gibb to postpone again their recording schedule, and Julio called off the concerts and television shows planned for England, West Germany, and Switzerland in early January.

For the next three weeks he lived in virtual seclusion with his mother close by. They tried not to speak of their fears. Julio later admitted, "My mother and I both knew that if one of us broke down, the other would, too."

Outwardly the household looked the same as usual. Anyone driving by would see the gardeners tending to the lush lawns that were highlighted by bright orange flowers, thick shrubs, and grapefruit trees. The real drama was going on inside the house, where Julio was pale and drawn.

The reporters who had clustered nearby hoping for daily bulletins abandoned their vigil. It was obvious that this was a tight-knit group. The leaks the press often elicits from fringe members of families caught up in dramatic events did not materialize; Julio's people had the situation under control.

No one on the inside was rude or unfriendly; Julio had always enjoyed good relations with the press, and he knew they had their job to do. But his first and only concern was to protect his beloved father with his silence.

Although he would give no hints about any efforts to find Dr. Iglesias, Julio did praise the kindness of his fans and admirers who had poured in messages of support. He was deeply touched by the Chilean schoolchildren who had taken the time to write him during the ordeal, and the group of Spanish parish women who let him know they were saying the rosary every morning for him and his father. More than twelve hundred letters a day were streaming in, a sign that Julio meant more to them than just a voice crooning love songs. He was overwhelmed by this evidence of public support.

He also could not help blaming himself for his father's situation; if it had not been for Julio's notoriety, Dr. Iglesias would be safe instead of the target of what the police now feared were experienced terrorists. According to Spanish officials, they could not immediately identify the kidnappers, but all signs led to a terrorist organization which often resorted to kidnapping as a means of getting attention and money.

Interpol, the international police force, was called in. They were able to sketch a composite picture of the kidnappers, and every day the Madrid police were questioning dozens of suspects. Carlos and Julio were in constant contact, thankful that the abduction was getting the highest priority in Spain.

On the Miami front, Julio said nothing about the latest developments. The story dried up as far as U.S. papers were concerned. But behind the scenes there was a flurry of activity directed at freeing Dr. Iglesias.

The family has gone on record as denying that a ransom had been demanded at any time by the kidnappers. Inside sources have said, however, that a ransom was indeed asked for the doctor—two million dollars, one million to be paid in dollars, the other million in pesetas. Dr. Iglesias' Madrid attorney told reporters at one point that he had been contacted on January 7 and had been warned that if the money was not paid, the doctor would be turned over to the ETA, the Basque separatist organization. By then, supposedly, Julio had received the demand in Miami.

Later that week it was said that one million dollars drawn from Julio's Miami bank was flown to Madrid, where one million in pesetas was already waiting. Everyone agrees, however, that not one cent of this money ever wound up in the hands of the terrorists.

Working swiftly and secretly, the Spanish police made every effort to find the doctor before any money changed hands. The big break came on January 17. A crack team of police specialists questioned several separatist suspects in northern Spain. One of those suspects was said to have broken under pressure and revealed the kidnappers' hideout.

According to the suspect, Dr. Iglesias was being held in the village of Trasmoz, a tiny community of some 180 people about 90 miles from Zaragoza, one of Spain's biggest cities. Without delay, more than a hundred armed police moved into position outside the suspects' house.

At the crack of dawn an anti-terrorist squad blasted its way into the hideout, dynamiting down the door and throwing in smoke grenades to confuse the kidnappers. The well-planned, perfectly executed rescue resulted in the capture of three men and one woman believed to be Basque separatists. Dr. Iglesias indeed was inside, slightly bewildered and deliriously happy to meet his rescuers.

Julio's father was sporting a nineteen-day growth of beard, but otherwise was in good condition, as Carlos, who had followed the operation every step of the way, was able to explain to Julio later that day.

Julio remembers that moment very well. "When I heard

my father's voice on the telephone I was so choked I could not talk," he said. "The first news of his release came from my brother . . . and right after that the Spanish presidential palace called. Then the phone rang and it was my father."

At the afternoon press conference Dr. Iglesias recalled his own reaction to the morning's rescue actions. He was asleep in the early dawn, he said, when "I heard a noise, then two more, all within five seconds, and suddenly a policeman opened the door and said I was free. I couldn't believe it."

Dr. Iglesias reported that the actual kidnapping nearly three weeks before had been done so quickly and efficiently that he had had no time to react. Seized at gunpoint, he had been threatened with death "unless you cooperate," then pushed into the trunk of a car and driven for nearly thirty-six hours before entering the hideout. He had passed the next eighteen days in the house, locked up with no contact with the outside world. He had been treated decently, although he complained that he had not been allowed to bathe or even change his clothes. Finally, in answer to his complaints, Dr. Iglesias said the abductors had bought him a shirt, but "they made me pay for it."

A thankful Julio said in Miami, "I wish it had been me instead of my father." He was grateful to the president of Spain and his ministers who had taken such a personal interest in the case. But he could not explain why the kidnappers, who were positively identified as part of the political-military wing of the ETA, had chosen his father. It was probably nothing more sinister than because of the family's wealth. In ten years ETA terrorists had been responsible for nearly forty kidnappings. Five of the victims had been killed, so Julio had much to be thankful for, as his father had survived. While the Iglesiases pointedly steered clear of Spanish politics, they of course knew that the ETA claims to be fighting to liberate Basque lands from Spain to form their own independent country.

Carlos tried to play down the politics of the situation, denying that as a motivation for the incident. "I didn't find out the kidnappers belonged to ETA until the Interior minister told me this morning, when my father was freed," he said. And he also emphasized that his father had not mentioned knowledge of the group's motives either. "When I first saw my father," he said, "he only gave me a kiss and said nothing."

They have continued to maintain ignorance of any underlying motives behind Dr. Iglesias' kidnapping, but the abduction changed their life-style. Afterward Dr. Iglesias gave up his medical practice, a proud profession that had given him much satisfaction for more than forty years. Fearful of being taken again, for the next couple of years he would not live in any one place for more than two weeks at a time, and roamed the world instead.

Carlos was anxious to get his father out of Spain and home to Julio. But before he left, ever the gracious Spanish aristocrat, the doctor wanted to fulfill his obligation to his saviors, so he hosted an expensive dinner in Madrid for the police officials who had risked their lives for him.

Then he joined Julio in Miami, where his happy family received him with joy. All Julio wanted was to give his father a sense of safety and peace again. The two spent a leisurely day on Julio's yacht, where they could relax and talk in complete privacy.

And for the first time in years Julio put aside all his career plans and took his mother, his father, and his children on an extended vacation. The only reminder of the bizarre kidnapping is in the tight ring of security that now accompanies Julio, whether he is traveling or staying at home. His bodyguards are discreet and not easy to spot, but he goes nowhere without them. There are compensations even here, though, since one of them is a shapely young Asian beauty, an expert in martial arts.

Home again, Julio concentrated on his career with new intensity. Now more than ever he wanted to make it in the United States, one of the safest countries in the world and popular with many wealthy foreigners who prefer its many protections to those in their native lands. Julio determined to redouble his efforts to break into this new market. But from what he had learned since moving to the States, sometimes talent was not enough. It would take a carefully controlled campaign to introduce him to this overcrowded buyers' market. Nothing must be left to chance. Julio would make a big splash even if he had to pay a high price for it; it would be worth every penny once he succeeded. And Julio never had doubts about his eventual success; he had never failed.

·7·

The Packaging of a Superstar

By 1982 Julio had been living in the United States more than three years but the usual reaction when his name was mentioned outside Hispanic circles was still "Julio who?" Everywhere else it was one of his most successful periods. His album *De Niña a Mujer,* the title song of which was dedicated to his own lovely daughter, Chaveli, had sales of two million in Brazil alone and more than one million in Japan.

When he toured Brazil, more than eighty thousand fans jammed the Flamingo Stadium in Rio de Janeiro for a concert. The best news came from England. There his version of "Begin the Beguine" broke onto the charts and spiraled to number one in a matter of weeks.

On the strength of that success, a five-concert stand was set up with Julio for the Royal Albert Hall in London. The English were completely charmed by Julio's satin-smooth voice and spectacular show. All five concerts were sellouts, with the bulk of his audience, as one bystander wrote, women "of all ages, shapes, and sizes," who acted like lovestruck teenagers vying for a rock idol's attention as they "made their way to the front of the stage, clutching bouquets of flowers. Once in position they threw either their gifts or themselves at their bronzed hero, and at one point almost overwhelmed his clutch of protective security guards."

Julio was gratified by the reception, but not half as much as CBS Records was. The campaign was beginning to pay off in the English-speaking market. And his enhanced image was also paying big dividends in Europe and Latin America, where he was bigger than ever. In Paris a museum dedicated a life-size statue of him for permanent exhibition. And CBS International Records awarded him their Crystal Globe Award, honoring him as their best-selling recording artist.

But Julio was still dissatisfied. The United States had been hospitable to him and curious about his talent, but he could not seem to master the language as well as he thought he should before releasing a U.S. record. He finally admitted that the United States is a territory different from any he'd known anywhere else in the world. It is a massive country and fragmented into diverse groups. Breaking into the top radio stations is difficult, as they confine almost all their play to established stars. Of course, with the heavy backing of CBS, Julio had a good chance of getting his songs played. But strong persuasion from an important label, even CBS, would not be enough. Newcomers spend a lot of time touring the nation to introduce their debut singles to the disc jockeys personally, giving interviews and making themselves known to influential people in the music media.

In spite of his concentrated English-language studies, Julio did not feel competent enough to take on the U.S. press. It was hard to understand how a man who could learn a language as complex as Japanese could have so much trouble with English. But, then, he had no plans to live in Japan and knew only enough to get by; Americans expected more.

As a Hispanic, naturally, he still thought first in his native language, Spanish. And he had no difficulty with the other Romance languages. "When I'm singing in any Latin language, Spanish, French, Italian, Portuguese," he said, "I'm growing up with that language. In school I studied French as a basic foreign language. I never studied English." The difficulty, he added, was not just in learning pronunciation, but the essence, the meaning of the words. "I just became conscious of how important the English was to the music when I started to sing. The lines feel different, the phrasing, the musical moods."

Julio was also learning how important it was to establish his name as a superstar in the United States. One aspect of the business as important as talent is a performer's public image. Through the years Hollywood has actually manufactured personalities, packaging novices who will give up everything, including their own names and identities, for a chance at stardom.

But not all such packaged stars have been successful. To be sure, all of them have stood in the limelight for a time, but the public has made the final decision, basing it on a star's natural warmth and personality rather than the created image. That explains why a kid named Roy Scherer, Jr., could make a lifelong career as Rock Hudson, and how Bernard Schwartz could last three decades as Tony Curtis, while others from their era and studios, who also underwent name changes and were pushed with the same publicity campaigns, rarely made more than two or three films. Or why a Brian Epstein could mold four lads from Liverpool (replacing one who did not fit the style he was creating) into the Beatles and immortality, while the mighty American Broadcasting Company failed when it tried to re-create that success with a group called the Bay City Rollers.

What it all proves is that a well-packaged entertainer can get enough media coverage to merit a hearing from the public. But from then on, talent or an exceptional personal-

ity must take over. Julio was sure he had demonstrated his
star appeal; now he needed to be properly introduced to
the American people.

There are any number of successful public relations
firms operating out of California and New York that have
helped create stars or that protect the images of superstars.
But one agency has led the pack for the last twenty years.
With a client list that reads like the Who's Who of Hollywood royalty, Rogers & Cowan is considered the premier
public relations firm in show business. Through the wisdom, talent, and energy of its founders, Henry Rogers and
Warren Cowan, the agency has opened offices all over the
globe, from its principal outlets in New York and Los Angeles to Washington, D.C., London, Paris, and wherever
the rich, famous, and glamorous need their assistance.

Good public relations people are on call twenty-four
hours a day, ready at the slightest hint of crisis to roll a
press release out of the typewriter to explain away trouble
or to smooth the client over the rough spots. They are the
ones who are expected to shape and control every word
written about the star. They have lists of just about every
writer on newspapers and magazines, large and small, and
an agency such as Rogers & Cowan can, when necessary,
get space for total unknowns or subtly influence the way a
story or crisis is handled, just because of their client list. If
a writer wants to get to a blockbuster star, the way can be
smoothed or obstructed by the PR agent, which gives that
company clout in helping lesser names; it is called a trade-
off.

Since Julio wants only the best of everything, naturally he
chose R & C as his publicists. He was in good company;
other stars who have used R & C include Robert Wagner,
Kate Jackson, Dudley Moore, and Cher, among others. Because R & C is so good, it is also extremely expensive, but
money was no object in Julio's case.

Rogers & Cowan's mission was clear: to make Julio Iglesias a household name in the United States. Of course, they agreed with CBS Records that it was imperative to get an English-language album onto the market. It is always easier to sell a known commodity than an abstract, and to Main Street U.S.A. the smiling Spaniard was a big zero. His heavy accent was definitely a drawback, as it seemed to make him uncomfortable around American reporters. But the pluses outweighed the minuses. Iglesias' good looks, charm and talent were all in his favor, and he could be sold to America as a proven winner, the number-one international singing superstar. This was sure to pique curiosity, and it was a natural for feature story space in the media.

The public relations firm wasted no time in mapping out a campaign that would package Julio Iglesias in an attractive way and position him among the top-ranking American stars. Meanwhile, Julio would do his part by improving his English and striving to get his U.S. LP ready for release.

First, it was important to introduce Julio properly to Hollywood, to the stars and moguls who are the movers and shakers of the industry. Iglesias was not exactly an unknown, having mingled with the celebrity crowd for several years, but he was famous more for his elegance and wealth than for his talent.

Topnotch public relations firms often intertwine the affairs of their clients. Frequently they will prevail on one of their legendary names to appear at or even host a party for one of their rising clients, a sort of one-hand-washing-the-other business. In return, the "name" may get a big discount on the fees normally charged for PR services. Everybody loves a bargain, and since such fees can run as high as $15,000 a month or more, cut rates are attractive. For other affairs, an agency might promise a superstar for a fund raiser or big event with the proviso that they can also showcase some of their other clients at the gala. These are only some of the reasons why performers choose their PR agencies with such care. There is a lot more at stake than just finding someone to churn out well-written releases. People in power favor the powerful agencies, and the stars who want long careers know better than to fight the system.

Even without any product or project to promote, Rogers & Cowan was able to make Julio a media favorite. Afterward experts said that R & C's Iglesias campaign was "simply brilliant. Total blanket coverage. They called in every card they were owed."

The campaign was kicked off in Los Angeles in January 1983. One of their longtime clients, Kirk Douglas, was to be honored at a testimonial dinner. Douglas is one of the all-time Hollywood greats, a charter member of the "A" list in a town where status and one's place in the pecking order count more than the box office of your latest movie. He is also "old" Hollywood, one of the last remnants of the studio star system and part of the elite clique that can make or break newcomers socially.

With Douglas' approval, Rogers & Cowan arranged for Julio Iglesias to be the gala's surprise entertainment. It was a memorable night as Julio took the stage and earned a standing ovation after he sang his English hit "Begin the Beguine" in several languages. Even Julio, who was used to adulation after a performance, was overwhelmed by the reception.

He was especially pleased because he had invited a very special guest for the evening—his daughter, Chaveli, who had flown from Spain to be his date. And, like any eleven-year-old, she was happy for her father, but while he was captivating the crowd, Chaveli had her eye on another superstar there. With a smile, Julio had to admit his daughter was "quite excited," because this was "her first glamorous affair, and she's enthusiastic about meeting Gregory Peck."

Round two of the Iglesias crusade came later that month. Socialite Betsy Bloomingdale threw a party in honor of the American Ambassador to the Vatican, William Wilson, and his wife. Besides the famous faces from the film capital, there were a number of jet setters, as well as a goodly sprinkling of Washington, D.C., figures, including one of Betsy Bloomingdale's dearest friends, Nancy Reagan. Mrs. Reagan graciously recalled meeting Iglesias before and again complimented him on his performance.

Now that he had made the society and gossip columns linked to such important people, it was only natural that the Iglesias name would also show up in the tabloids. To be sure, the stars openly deplore the supermarket scandal sheets, but young hopefuls have been known to court their writers and photographers. After all, the tabloids reach millions of households every week, many of them homes in which other publications are not usually found—and their readers are great entertainment fans, buying records, watching TV, going to movies. As long as the stories do not harm their families or careers, most shrewd stars have learned to live with this sort of publicity.

The tidbits about Julio's private life that were leaked were not that different from what had appeared in the Hispanic press. And since his appeal is directed mainly toward women, he appreciated the interest in the fact that he sleeps in T-shirts and sweat pants, that his favorite colors are white and blue, and that he is a meticulous dresser who has made the best-dressed lists for more than ten years.

Stories appeared detailing Julio's awesome success in countries around the globe. It was hard for Americans to believe that a man with 680 gold records to his credit could be virtually unheard of in the United States. But interest was growing.

CBS International Records was ready to move. The company read the signs and believed the time had come for an assault on the U.S. marketplace by Latin singers. Besides Julio, they were promoting another Hispanic star, Camilo Sesto. In his favor, Sesto spoke and sang in impeccable English and was preparing an English-language album produced by Harry Maslin, who was responsible for many of the pop hits by the Australian band Air Supply.

A Venezuelan heartthrob, José Luis Rodríguez (El Puma), was also crossing over from the Spanish to the American scene. His appearances on Jerry Lewis' Muscular Dystrophy Telethon and Anne Murray's television special were well received. It was becoming a race to see which of the trio, if any, could capture the United States.

The other two may have been talented and poised, but Julio was the one with the acumen to use that high-powered press campaign as the centerpiece of his entrance into the United States. And that really made the difference.

With all the great media coverage, though, CBS International knew that they had to release something of Julio's soon. It was that or lose all the ground they had gained in introducing him. They finally put out *Julio,* an LP comprising his greatest hits, some in English, most in Spanish. At least with that on display, Julio could be a guest on TV talk shows, making him real to the public that knew him only from news stories. Julio sang a lot and talked a little with Merv Griffin on his show and repeated his performance for Johnny Carson on *The Tonight Show,* the most important outlet for any entertainer with a new project to sell.

Johnny Carson and David Letterman also were the ones who discovered a new source of humor by talking up the newcomer and then doing a double-take at the audience, asking, "Julio who?" It never failed to get a big laugh; the question became a standard joke in 1983. Nobody minded because it also kept Julio's name alive, which is the primary goal of any publicity campaign.

It was with the release of *Julio* that Iglesias started to

collect dividends on his expensive public relations invest-
ment. The album rang up sales of more than half a million
copies. Several of his previous hit Spanish albums were
shipped to the stores and also moved briskly.
Newsweek magazine climbed on the bandwagon, herald-
ing his arrival as an important star. "The most popular
singer in the world today isn't Mick Jagger or Kenny Rogers
or Paul McCartney or even Frank Sinatra," that much-
respected weekly exclaimed. "He's a . . . Spaniard named
Julio Iglesias, a master of the love song."

Meanwhile, the tabloids were trying to stir up a feud
between Iglesias and Johnny Carson, who had split recently
from his third wife, Joanna. Because Julio traveled in the
same circles as the Carsons and had been seen escorting
her to an affair or two, speculation began that Carson was
angry about the twosome and would henceforth keep Julio
off *The Tonight Show.* Carson is the absolute ruler of that
showcase, and he has now and again been rumored to ban
from that important outlet celebrities who have offended
him in some way. Even the most famous names in Hollywood have been known to get nervous about rubbing Carson the wrong way because one appearance on his show
with a new album or film clip can make the difference between failure and success. To his credit, however, Johnny
Carson is aware of his awesome power in the business and
uses his veto power sparingly.

A few weeks after the rumors about Julio and Joanna
Carson surfaced, Julio was again a guest on Johnny Carson's show. And when Julio was asked later about the romance, he denied any involvement, offering that favorite
Hollywood standby: we're just good friends.

Usually it is hard to tell just who Julio's romance of the
month is; his entourage includes at least half a dozen beautiful women at any time. He certainly was not living like a
monk, although he was learning to warn the ladies who

caught his fancy not to expect a lasting relationship. He often said, "The more I look for that special woman to commit myself to, the more I don't seem to find her. I am constantly searching for true love, but in the end none of my relationships really seem to last."

When Giannina Facio walked into his life, friends could not help but notice how much she resembled Isabel. Dark, with brown hair, Giannina, the daughter of a Costa Rican diplomat, met Julio in Miami, and she struck a spark in him. Giannina wanted to be a model, but she was willing to postpone her career to follow the sun with Julio.

But Julio could think of little else but his career, a tendency that can put a damper on love affairs. Since neither had any illusions when they went into the romance, neither was disillusioned when it was over. He has only the fondest memories of their time together, calling it "a short love story. She's truly sensational, a beautiful creature." However, he is quick to add, "I never thought of marrying her," although "this episode has left me with pleasant memories."

The parting was on the best of terms. They still see each other and talk. Giannina, a young woman not yet jaded or sophisticated in the ways of love, worries about her dear friend. "I wish him much happiness and spiritual peace," she says of Julio, because this "is what he needs most."

She looks back on their affair as a learning experience, calling it "a pretty adventure because I never saw the possibility of a commitment. I learned a lot about famous men and their attitudes toward women and love." But because Julio was open and honest with her, his attitude did not embitter her. Instead she insists, "I sincerely hope that he will someday find his soul mate. I know he will."

So far Julio seems to have found only one soul mate that he embraces with passion—his music. Beautiful women drift through his life like clouds, first light, airy, beautiful to contemplate, then, with time, darker, full of storm warnings, until they disappear. Women are hard to understand, and if they feel neglected, they can walk out, which can be a serious blow to the Iglesias ego. Giannina observed that Julio "is obsessed with women falling in love with him, and he doesn't understand why a woman might wish to leave him."

Music is much easier to understand, and it is his to control, which may be why it is his true mistress. Whenever he was bored with the constant success of his compositions and recordings, he could create new challenges, new risks to get his adrenaline flowing again. That was one reason why the United States was so important to him—he would be flirting with danger, with failure.

"When you start to work," Julio says, "you're hungry and excited. Later, after you've climbed some, it's your legs and emotions that get tired. Now I have half of my career to go. To work in this country is going to take years off my life, but it's the biggest mountain of all, and one that I must climb."

Meanwhile, the publicity campaign was easing his climb. The fact that he was single was an added attraction, as a strong part of the plan was to emphasize Julio's sex appeal. He was billed as one of the world's most eligible bachelors and a man who delighted in the company of women. But, while the press was always on the lookout for new pairings and tried to keep pace with his entanglements, Julio preferred to be known as a gentleman rather than a Lothario. He was always gracious when he remembered old flames, and as discreet as possible about current ones.

When pressed for details of his love life, he sighed, "Sometimes I wake up alone. Sometimes I don't wake up alone. It's the same life as everybody's." At times he seemed embarrassed by the intimate turn interviews could take, but he was never rude. At other times he was a bit disgusted by people probing into his private affairs instead of asking about his music. The constant glare of publicity surrounding his women may have prompted the outburst when he told a reporter, "Look, I've never killed anybody. I don't take drugs. I lead a quiet life, and I'm certainly not Superman. . . . Listen, I'm tired of the stereotypical macho-man legend. . . . I'm a man who loves women, life, the sun, sports, and my solitude."

Yet he continued to allow himself to be packaged and sold as a Latin lover. Facing the tough competition around him, Julio was confident that he would emerge victorious in the Spanish sweepstakes because he paid the most attention to the details that lead to success. "A singer has to sell his personality," he said. "That is more important than even his music." And his personality was being sold not only through his records and personal appearances, but through the news media. It was a two-pronged attack, a surefire approach.

What he really needed to do now was devote himself to the English-language album that was always being promised but never produced. Yet before he could proceed, he had a tour lined up, one that would again be directed at his loyal Latin fans, but would now, he hoped, also draw "the Saxons" on the strength of his *Julio* release.

The one thing Julio refused to alter was his concert style. Proud of the fact that he was popular due to his throbbing voice, a carefully modulated instrument, he has worked for years to develop it and is constantly improving. And his fans know an Iglesias concert will be polished and pleasing to the eye and ear. He spurns the usual sex-oriented strutting other singers employ to send their fans into rapturous frenzies. "I don't dance around or jump up and down onstage," he says. "I don't use my body to manipulate people."

For all the fans he has made with his coolly sensual style, Julio also has his critics, viewers who are bored by his precise control and utter lack of movement. Americans especially, raised on the splash and flash of teen idols, may find an Iglesias concert bland, unless they're older women turned on by his quiet blend of romance and restrained passion.

The Latin community has no problem understanding Julio's understated performance. In reviewing one of his New York concerts, *Billboard*'s Latin critic advised that "in any language Julio's complete control of the voice is astonishing. And his restrained stage presence, which borders on stiffness and timidity, forced the spectators to concentrate all their attention on that remarkable instrument."

But while his style pleased them and they respected the fact that he would not change it to please his new audience, that the Latin flavor would remain, there were the first rumblings of dissent from the Hispanics about their idol's crossing over to the Anglo-Americans. On his concert swing, Julio was scheduled for a few nights in Los Angeles at the Universal Amphitheatre. This was the first tour in which he was also adding English-language songs to his standard repertoire.

In Los Angeles, of course, he drew quite a few new fans from mainstream America, especially on opening night. But when he turned his attention to them, bantering with them and singing in English, it angered certain segments on the Hispanic side. Several fans shouted rudely for him to sing more Spanish. Caught by surprise, Julio tried to be gracious, explaining that he had a more international crowd these days at his concerts and he owed it to them to sing their songs. When the heckling continued, Julio suggested, in Spanish, that his Hispanic fans come back another night "when the Americans aren't here," and he promised to do more of their favorites. It was an unsettling moment for Julio.

But most of the fans remained loyal, while the new ones showed their appreciation in typical American style. Latin performers in the United States often remark on the energy and enthusiasm of American audiences; Americans like to participate in the performance. In other countries happy fans applaud wildly and sway in their seats to the rhythms or come to the front to throw flowers at Julio's feet. He was unprepared for the wave of response he received when "the Saxon" ladies turned out. They rushed the stage and had to be physically restrained by his bodyguards. Others threw such intimate objects as panties at his feet—or their hotel keys.

It was more than the gentleman singer from Spain could take. He admitted in his charming Spanish voice: "I am embarrassed by these displays. I never see myself as a sex symbol. . . . I am not more good lover than a normal man." Julio sees himself as just "a good salesman . . . I sell dreams."

He also learned that certain women make the concert circuit the same as the stars, only their performances are much more private. These girls like to go to bed with the stars. They don't even expect a real relationship; to many it is a game, and they exchange lists and ratings to see who has slept with the biggest superstars—and how they stack up against the others. One infamous groupie in the 1970s started her own private collection of personal memorabilia from her conquests—somehow she talked them into letting her mold casts of their private parts! But Julio prefers to meet his women through friends. He is aware of the effect his singing has on the opposite sex, which makes him very considerate. Says he, "I do not take advantage. I don't like groupies."

It was about the middle of 1983 that Julio decided to cut down on his tours and concentrate on his U.S. album. But there was one opportunity he could not pass up. Club de Vacaciones, a travel organization, wanted to sponsor an Iglesias tour of Spain and Portugal. The cost would be in the neighborhood of two to three million dollars because he would be traveling with a full complement of one hundred musicians, technicians, and bodyguards, so he would not see much profit from the concerts, but he felt it had been too long since he had entertained in his native land.

The truth is, there had never been the same clamoring for Julio in Spain that he experienced everywhere else in Hispania. Central America, South America, Puerto Rico, Mexico—these were the hot spots for his talents, but his first youthful hits aside, Julio was unappreciated in his own country.

Right from the moment he landed at the Madrid airport, however, Julio sensed a decided change in his countymen's attitude toward him. Perhaps his rising fame in the United States had given him better status or instilled a new spirit of pride in his accomplishments in the Spanish people, for he was mobbed by fans when he stepped off his plane. Obviously moved by this outburst, he admitted he was delighted to be "rediscovered" by the people he loved best. In the course of the next month he performed in a series of standing-room-only concerts in the biggest soccer stadiums in Madrid, Barcelona, and other major cities.

The highlight of the tour came in the resort town Palma de Mallorca, where he gave a dazzling benefit concert before Spain's King Juan Carlos and Queen Sophia. This Royal Gala had sold out, with the tickets priced from $66 to $100, very high by that poor country's standards. Everywhere else the tickets ranged from $6 to $26, but Julio was honored and humbled by the fact that he could raise so much money to help the less fortunate, and he was glad to give this benefit performance.

It was one of Spain's major events; so was the entire tour. The critics raved, the fans raved. Several of the concerts were carried live over Spain's biggest radio network. Overjoyed, Julio said good-bye to Spain but vowed to return soon.

From Spain, he was expected to fly to Portugal for two concerts, but at the last minute he had to bow out. He had run into the most difficult obstacle international stars face—currency laws. Unlike the United States, many nations have stringent rules that keep their money from leaving the country. The poorer nations especially keep a sharp eye on entertainers, sports figures, and other big money-makers earning large sums within their borders. Since Julio's sold-out concert before 30,000 at Lisbon's Restelo Stadium was expected to earn him some $290,000, there were permits that had to be officially issued in order for him to transfer that much money out of the country. The permits had not been issued, so, reluctantly, Julio canceled the concert. He also had to cancel a benefit concert that would have raised the same amount for the League Against Cancer. That was the low spot of the tour, but there was nothing he could do about it.

By the end of the tour in early September, Julio's triumph had been well reported in the press. Rogers & Cowan was continuing the media blitz on this Spanish phenomenon and already were planning new campaign strategies to keep his face and name in the columns.

September marked another milestone in Julio's life; it was going to be his fortieth birthday. The "Big 0" birthdays—30, 40, and 50—have come to be regarded as milestones, to be celebrated with special enthusiasm, sometimes tinged with desperation.

Julio is one who both loves and hates the passing years.

There is a confidence that comes only from experience, an improved ability to deal with life. But there are also subtle physical changes. The senses are less acute, and the years bring a keener awareness of how precious life itself is because it must someday end for all of us, rich and poor, the strong as well as the weak.

With all the riches and sweetness in his world—the women, cars, homes, fans, adoration, success—Julio knows it is all fleeting. The specter of death is always with him, perhaps because he came so close to it when he had his accident. "I want to die very, very, very late," he says. "I want . . . my life . . . for a long time—a hundred years is okay."

But birthdays mean parties, and in show business, parties mean publicity. Julio spent his actual birthday quietly on the island of Sardinia, working on his tan and putting the final touches to his plans for the still elusive American record.

In the meantime Rogers & Cowan had constructed a truly spectacular event to coincide with Julio's birthday. The Guinness Book of Records was informed of Julio's international recording achievements, 100 million albums sold in six languages, definitely a world record.

Here was a perfect coupling of two interesting show business phenomena. Julio was a hot personality, sure to merit plenty of publicity from any award the Guinness people gave him. Thus the Diamond Disc Award, given to singers who have sold 100 million albums, was invented. Other superstars might have walls lined with the official gold and platinum records awarded by the recording industry, but only Julio could now boast a Diamond Disc. It was a great ego booster for him, just what he needed as he reached forty.

Both parties to this award were eager to wring as much news mileage as possible out of it. Paris was selected for the ceremony, for many reasons. First, it is an international center and guaranteed access to many of Julio's renowned personal friends. Second, it assured plenty of acceptances from news people, who were invited on an all-expenses-paid junket to report on this new and important award. Last, it had been arranged that another impressive honor was to be bestowed on Julio the same day—the Medal of the City of Paris. It was one of those rare moments when a chain of events come together for a public relations firm and they can get double coverage for the price of one party. Once again it was evident that Julio Iglesias was born under a lucky star.

The Paris adventure was a spectacle he will never forget. The Diamond Disc was a work of art—a gold record studded with magnificent diamonds. It came with a plaque commemorating his achievement. As for the Médaille de Vermeil de la Ville de Paris, he and a roomful of friends were visibly moved when the Mayor of Paris conferred the honor on Julio in a ceremony that took place in the historic, memory-filled Paris City Hall.

Magazine and newspaper reporters from all over were on hand to witness the bestowing of the awards, and later they joined Julio and his friends at a party in his honor at the Pre Catelan restaurant. He was properly surprised when waiters rolled out a birthday cake for him, and he graciously acknowledged that he was now forty. Among the guests were singer Donna Summer and actresses Jane Seymour, Ursula Andress, Pam Dawber, and Leslie Caron. Director Roman Polanski also congratulated Julio, along with a very happy, smiling Walter Yetnikoff, president of CBS Records. Julio was especially delighted by the appearance of two dear friends, Regine, the famed café owner, and her husband, Roger. Whenever Julio is in New York, Regine's is his favorite watering hole.

When he returned to the United States, there was another party awaiting him, this time in New York, hosted by Regine and Roger. And Julio had more fun at it than anyone else. When he arrived at Regine's at 10 P.M., things were just heating up. He was dancing as Liza Minnelli came through the door, and before the other guests knew what was happening, Julio and Liza were starting to sizzle on the dance floor. Cheering them on were Charles Aznavour and Plácido Domingo and his wife, Marta.

The world-renowned Spanish tenor and Julio have been friends for many years and have even sung together in concert and on a television special. So it was no wonder that Domingo would not miss a party for Julio, even though he had given a strenuous five-hour performance of *Les Troyens* at the Metropolitan Opera that same night. He added his powerful voice to the others when another birthday cake was rolled out for Julio and everyone sang "Happy Birthday."

Others might have been exhausted by the constant round of parties, but the activity seemed to make Julio more energetic. He was content that wherever he looked, his face was in the papers or he was being quoted. Without a single American product, he had become a superstar, even if many of his admirers did not have the foggiest notion what he did for a living.

Now that he had been packaged into a famous commodity, however, he knew time was running out. If he did not complete that U.S. album, he would be forgotten as quickly as yesterday's news. Besides, it was time to settle down a bit, put off future tours, and really concentrate on this amazing and frightening new market.

Julio told his associates that he would henceforth stop "every concert all over the world" until he had the material in place for the U.S. record. He still spent time doing television shows—Merv Griffin and *The Tonight Show,* as well as the syndicated hit music showcase *Solid Gold*—but the rest of the time he lived like a recluse and spent long nights at the studio.

Once his mind was made up, Julio brought a sense of urgency to the project. It was an attitude very familiar to his associates. One of them has said that Julio is never satisfied. "He always wants more—more love, more hours, more records, more success."

He is, according to his personal press manager, always in a hurry. And when he sets his mind to something, nothing can stand in his way; he must have what he wants no matter what the cost. "Everything has to be quick for Julio," this close business associate claims. The best example he has of Julio's impatience happened when the singer decided the water in his Miami pool was too hot. "I offered to turn down the thermostat," his friend says, "but he said that would take too long. We had trucks dump five tons of ice into the pool."

With that kind of decisiveness, Julio plunged into the U.S. project. Promises were made; CBS would have his LP in a matter of months!

·8·

"To All the Girls I've Loved Before"

*B*ecause of all the delays there had been with the record, Barry Gibb was no longer available to produce it. In the pop and rock recording industry the producer is as important as the vocalist. It is the producer who is on top of the latest popular industry sound and who adapts and develops that sound to fit the singer's skills and range. Many top composer/singers, among them Gibb and Barry Manilow, also hire out as producers.

Julio was fortunate that he could persuade Richard Perry to climb aboard and produce. Perry has been a standout in the rock style for more than a decade and has an ear to the top-10 sound. Julio and Perry formed a mutual admiration society, although Perry mainly worked on the cuts featuring Julio's American friends, while the solos were still supervised by Julio's trusted friend and co-worker Ramón Arcusa. He trusts Arcusa to mold the satiny Iglesias sound that has made him famous, and it is a trust born of long hours together in the studio and the kind of results that earned Julio the Diamond Disc.

Perry and many of Julio's other mentors knew that if he was to succeed with the same degree of popularity he experienced everywhere else, the album would need a hook, something extraordinary that would get the attention of disc jockeys—and then the audience.

Once again the Iglesias luck came to his rescue. Another one of the CBS recording stable, one of its supersuccessful superstars, indicated an interest in doing something with Julio. Willie Nelson's wife had heard Julio in London on the radio and thought his voice would complement Willie's. Julio was ecstatic. Willie Nelson had also crossed over from his original musical domain, country and western, into middle of the road, a much broader category. Now he was king of both divisions.

Julio could not have agreed more with Willie's wife's opinion, either. He could blend in with Willie; after all, his Spanish love songs were only "little stories," similar to the love stories behind most country hits.

It was easy to seal the deal with Willie. Both were CBS artists, so they decided to exchange duets on their forthcoming albums. This, everyone then realized, was the hook Julio needed to get attention. He would alternate solos, offering his own new material with duets with other established American superstars.

From then on, the album just fell into place. Julio sought out Diana Ross, who, he says, has been "a personal friend for many years." At parties and various affairs they had often duetted, and Julio recalls they "were happy singing a song together and one day I said, 'When are we going to record?' " Then they found "All of You" and put it on both their albums.

Next he contacted the Beach Boys, who were scattered around California. They had recorded together only sporadically in the 1980s, but the opportunity of mixing it up with a Latin superstar interested them.

Richard Perry was enthusiastic about the way the LP was shaping up. It would be simple working with the Beach

Boys in the studio, and he believed that the combination of old stars with the new assured the LP of much more radio air plays than if Julio was featured alone.

Radio stations, until the arrival of Music Television (MTV), traditionally have been the only way new artists can break into the business. This gives the disc jockeys more power over the industry than anyone likes to admit. In the 1960s the payola scandals were eye-openers concerning the DJ's control over artists and labels. Many DJs were given cars, women, money, and anything else they wanted in exchange for air time with new releases. Even the superstars were dependent on the DJs; if the records were not heard on the air, no one knew they were in the stores.

Times have changed; stations have policies against really notorious gratuities finding their way to DJs, but this tiny handful of opinion makers still picks the hits. And competition is so fierce that the top-40 stations play it safe, sticking with proven talent as much as possible. New artists need a gimmick to get the ears of the hit makers. But anything from Willie Nelson, Diana Ross, or the Beach Boys automatically makes the playing lists. At least while the songs were being introduced, Julio would just be along for the ride.

Richard Perry insisted it was a fair exchange, claiming "the duets [with Nelson and Ross] give us an instant ear in the area of the public that would have taken years to penetrate. As for the American artists, Julio's giving them an international platform that they may never have gotten on their own."

Since both Americans had been favorites on the charts in dozens of foreign countries, where American music is the rage, this may have been news to them and their managers. Not that it mattered. As the project progressed, it worked miracles for everyone involved.

Julio and Willie chose one new number, "To All the Girls

I've Loved Before," and one old standby, "As Time Goes By," for their joint efforts. Actually, "To All the Girls . . ." was not really new. It was written in the 1970s for Frank Sinatra, but for some reason he never heard it and the song had been shelved until Julio and Willie heard it and realized its potential. The two traveled to Willie's territory, Austin, Texas, to record. Willie's wife had been right; they clicked right away as a team. Pleased to be duetting with one of America's most beloved singers, Julio admitted he was one of the former "Outlaw's" greatest fans.

"He's the most natural singer in the world," Julio said, "completely spontaneous. With my voice, everything is happening in my tummy." He was equally complimentary of his sessions with Diana Ross. "You believe everything she says," he announced. CBS was so excited by what they heard that it was decided that, even without the album ready for release, they would send one of the duets out as a single. Plans were also made to shoot videos with Willie and Diana.

MTV has wrought many innovations in music. Video cassettes had been around for more than ten years but were basically confined to video jukeboxes in record stores and department stores where teenagers gathered. No one could guess the dynamic impact videos would have on the industry until a twenty-four-hour all-video music station was beamed on cable TV. It was as if the business had been electrically charged. MTV became the most important medium for new releases.

With MTV providing a steady outlet for video cassettes, there was a boom in their production. Then, in 1983, Michael Jackson hit the charts with the *Thriller* album, and after the first two singles, "Beat It" and "Billie Jean," debuted on MTV, there was no going back. Overnight stations canceled programming in their prime young-adult time slots—4:30 to 6:00 P.M. and late-night Fridays and

Saturdays—to air video cassette shows. For the TV stations the new programming was an ideal situation. The cassettes were usually provided free by the record companies, lowering broadcasting costs to nearly zero. And their ratings zoomed for the next year.

Recording artists were carefully monitoring the new marketing tool, and it was imperative to release video cassettes along with the LPs. Julio was happy to go along with it, since he is very photogenic. He and Willie just had fun translating their song to film. With Diana there was a sense of animal magnetism between her and Julio that made the song even hotter than on the platter.

During the long months he spent perfecting the album, Julio was full of energy. He is so intense about maintaining his position in show business, so jealous of the younger artists challenging his supremacy that he seems liveliest when he is trying to create a hit that will outsell all previous hits. The women who surround him and the possessions stardom has earned him mean little to him. He confesses, "The only thing exciting to me is when I am in the studio recording."

But the strategy behind his assault on the American public was to make Julio very visible. In the 1960s blanket coverage would have been possible by having him appear as a guest on the many variety hours then on television. But by 1983 there was not a single weekly musical hour on TV, and even variety specials were reserved for holiday viewing.

The choice spots now for singers were those rare specials and the many music industry award shows. At least once a month one or another music association or industry publication seems to present plaques or statuettes to the top artists via television programs, with many of the acts performing live. Performers are always willing to attend because the shows do extremely well in the ratings.

Although he still did not have an English-language record in the stores, Julio found it easy to be booked on TV specials, thanks to his strong publicity campaign. Since he cut an elegant figure in Washington society, he was a natural for a holiday TV special being taped there. The theme was "Christmas in Washington," and the intention was to show off the city's far-reaching international community. With embassies from nearly every nation, from the mightiest to the tiniest, along with America's own federal government, Washington occupies a unique place. The TV show aimed to demonstrate that although nations may speak different languages and embrace different cultures, all are united by the common need for peace and human decency. Certainly there was no better star for such a special than Julio.

With President Reagan and other Washington dignitaries in the audience, Julio sang the American favorite "White Christmas" with the show's host, Andy Williams, then sang "Winter Wonderland" with a chorus of children. Finally, in keeping with the spirit of the show, he sang "Silent Night," not just in English, but in German and Spanish as well.

Julio was not ashamed to admit that he was nervous before the show. This was not an informal talk show or *Solid Gold,* but what amounted to an American command performance with the President in attendance. And he knew that in a few days the special would be beamed to the country—his prime-time debut in America. "It is the *most* difficult thing I ever did in my life," he admitted, "because it is the most American thing I ever did."

Fortunately, the show and Julio were well received. But he still was not satisfied with his English pronunciation. He had second thoughts about another thoroughly American appearance that his mentors had pulled off for him—to sing the National Anthem at the Super Bowl in January.

By appearing at one of the year's highest-rated events and one that draws a mostly male viewership, Julio would be broadening his appeal. Of course, "The Star Spangled Banner" is considered a killer in the fraternity of singers, and perhaps someone recalled what happened when Robert Goulet sang it at a championship boxing match: he forgot the words. Pleading prior commitments, Julio begged off the Super Bowl.

But he eagerly agreed to sing with Willie Nelson at the Country Music Awards. CBS was ready to launch their single "To All the Girls I've Loved Before," and there was no better prime-time space than the Country Music Association's show. Willie was red-hot with his "Always on My Mind" number-one hit, so his appearance assured the CMA of a huge audience.

Then the twosome, looking like the odd couple, were introduced and eased into the number. It brought down the house. Within days of its release, "To All the Girls I've Loved Before" was getting exceptionally heavy radio play. *Cashbox,* the industry's most important publication, put the song in their Adult Contemporary category, and in reviewing it said: "Nelson gives the tune his traditional Texas flavor, while Julio adds a sexy Latin touch to the song. The pair dedicated the song to all the women in their past in a rich love ballad. Expect heavy A/C [Adult Contemporary] and country air play."

The heavy air play sent cash registers in record stores spinning, too, and the single entered the top-100 charts at number 80. On the Country top-100 it came in at number 66. There was no denying that Julio Iglesias had arrived, even if it was on the coattails of Willie Nelson.

Now he had a hit song, which made Julio truly newsworthy. As the single shot up to the top 10, where it lingered for many weeks, American women wanted to learn more about this handsome man with the Latin looks and smooth, sexy voice. Julio no longer had to seek out the press for interviews; the press was coming to him. Rogers & Cowan had promised that Julio Iglesias would be the star to watch in 1983 and, next to the skyrocketing Michael Jackson, he was the most exciting.

By now Julio also realized that American audiences, while politely interested in hearing about his international triumphs, were most interested in his experiences since his move to the States. And it was clear that his thick accent made him self-conscious. Because of it, he still limited his appearances. Admittedly, it also kept interfering with his recordings. Trying to go American, he confessed, caused nothing but "pain, pain, pain, because when I have the accent, sometimes I don't have the feeling, but when I have the feeling, the accent is not so good. So I have to repeat and repeat and repeat."

But his female fans did not seem to care about the accent; if anything, it endeared him to them. When his engagement at Atlantic City's Resorts International Hotel was announced, the gambling palace experienced the fastest sell-out in that town's history. This was particularly pleasing as Julio had invited several friends in Spain to fly over for his appearance; they were suitably impressed by his superstar suite in the hotel.

CBS was not resting on Julio's laurels, either. They again rushed out several of his old albums and were surprised at the unusually active cassette sales. The reason for that, according to his PR man, was the fact that "it became the 'in' thing with New York society to buy Julio cassettes. We got a lot of momentum going with that in New York." But even Rogers & Cowan was amazed at the Iglesias publicity blitz. "We never thought he would take off as he did," an executive exclaimed.

Busy as he was, Julio did not neglect his love life, which was picking up as his fame increased in America. Now women knew who he was when he looked their way. As always, he had an eye for youth and beauty.

Any rising star can find himself the object of beautiful women's advances in the show business capitals of Los Angeles, New York, London, Paris, Las Vegas, or wherever else the rich and famous gather to play. This time his roving eye connected with an eighteen-year-old model, Robin Smith, whom he met beside a swimming pool at one of Las Vegas' casino hotels. "She is so beautiful," he reportedly said to friends, and he quickly made his move. Robin was dazzled by his attentions. What girl wouldn't be? Julio is famous for sending his girls dozens of yellow roses and introducing them to a way of life straight out of the Arabian Nights. There were secret trysts in Miami and Lake Tahoe and Hollywood. But, like others before her, she found that as swiftly as her Prince Charming had swept her off her feet, he faded from her life. He was about to take off on a sixty-city tour, and it was business before pleasure as usual.

As "To All the Girls . . ." was waning on the charts, Julio's duet with Diana Ross, "All of You," was distributed, and again there was no doubt that it would go gold. Iglesias fever was rampant in America. Basking in the glow of this long-awaited fame, Julio happily exclaimed, "All over the world people are talking about what is going to happen with me. . . . The day I sing in Ohio in the summertime to ten thousand people, then I will be in America." While this sounded humble, there was no denying Julio's confidence that it was just a matter of time before that happened.

Besides, there were other lucrative paths for Julio to explore now that he had made his mark in English. The only rival he had for the top spot in the limelight was the slim, black, supertalented Michael Jackson. No one had made such an impact in the music business since the Beatles and Elvis. Michael Jackson was the king of the airwaves, with three songs simultaneously in the top 10, and two of the top-10 videos of the year. Julio Iglesias may have outsold him before, but the *Thriller* LP went beyond the usual superlatives of hit or megahit and coined a new phrase, "monster hit," to describe its worldwide sales. With that hot hit to his credit, Michael and his brothers signed one of the richest advertising deals in history, with Pepsi Cola. The very fact that Michael would be starring in the commercials made big headlines, and the filming of the television ads, by Bob Giraldi, the premier TV commercial director, reaped millions of dollars of free publicity for the soft drink company.

Pepsi's chief competitor in the soda wars was hard pressed to keep up in the superstar sweepstakes. Coca Cola cast about for a star of equal stature as their spokesman. These two corporations are engaged in a long-standing, fierce battle for the number-one spot in sales, and the Jackson deal was considered a great coup for Pepsi.

Not only was Michael extolling the virtues of his favorite soft drink, but Pepsi was also sponsoring the Jacksons' Victory Tour, then being touted as the most exciting musical extravaganza of all time.

When they looked over the roster of available superstars, undoubtedly Coca Cola was impressed by Rogers & Cowan's releases promising that Julio was the star to watch in 1983. Feelers were sent out; Julio expressed interest in taking on the task of hyping Coke.

Gossip columnists soon learned of the upcoming deal, and reports of its magnitude were discussed wherever show business people gathered. But negotiations did not go smoothly. In fact, the deal nearly turned into a fiasco when the first press conference, scheduled for early April 1984, at New York's Waldorf-Astoria, fell through. Both parties tried to downplay the incident. The press had received invitations, the ballroom was reserved, and a satellite network was set up to broadcast the press conference worldwide. There was no doubt that the conference was to announce Coca Cola's deal with Julio Iglesias. Then at what was reported as the eleventh hour, the Coca Cola company canceled everything. Rumor had it that there had been some last-minute haggling over money, that Julio wanted too much.

However, it was finally straightened out, and shortly thereafter the party went on as rescheduled. If there were any red faces over the previous problems, none were evident as the soft drink company proudly introduced Julio as their new spokesman.

The three-year deal was reported to be worth anywhere from $5 million to $20 million, with Julio making commercials for the soda corporation and having Coke sponsor his tours during this period. Tours are an integral part of the rock scene nowadays. Touring has become prohibitively expensive because of all the equipment necessary to mount the spectacular light and sound displays young fans have come to expect. Getting backing from a corporate sponsor guarantees a profit at the end. In return, the sponsor is liberally mentioned in the ads and write-ups, as well as on banners and other scenic decorations. Most companies looking to sell to the new preppies and yuppies believe identification with a pop personality offers the most effective entree to that market.

Coke, of course, realized that Julio's appeal was to a more mature crowd. Even though his singles were doing extremely well on the charts, most of the customers were women over twenty-five, but that was fine with Coke. That was precisely the audience they wanted for their Diet Coke, and Julio was scheduled to make a commercial for that product.

Besides, he would also be their primary representative in

the Hispanic world. To the Hispanic population in the United States, which currently totals more than fifteen million people, Julio is a leader, an idol. His ads on their networks would have the same impact for Coke that Michael Jackson had for Pepsi and the "Anglos."

A Pepsi Cola spokesman advised that their company was not worried about Coke's move. Julio, they believed, was not in the same league with their entertainers. "We think Julio Iglesias is a wonderful entertainer," the Pepsi person said. "But he is not Michael Jackson. And he is not Lionel Richie," another recent Pepsi ad recruit.

Fortunately, the rivalry between entertainers was limited to the press barrage. The players were actually on a much friendlier basis. And it was Julio who was chosen that year to hand out the Grammy for Album of the Year on that prestigious award show. It was no surprise when Coke's Iglesias handed the award to Pepsi's Jackson, since *Thriller* took most of that year's prizes.

Before he embarked on his sixty-city tour, which was expected to last from September 1984 until February 1985, CBS planned to get more of his material on the market. The album was set to be in the stores by late August, but while he waited for final confirmation on that, Julio was beset by another embarrassing happening, this one completely beyond his control.

When Julio recorded "To All the Girls I've Loved Before," he and Willie also sang "As Time Goes By," the classic from the 1940s movie masterpiece *Casablanca*. It was one of Julio's favorite songs and fit into Willie's repertoire too, as he had moved into singing pop standards. The second song was due to end up in one of Willie's next albums, but one not yet ready for release.

Somehow, the single of "As Time Goes By" was shipped to record stores. Confused retailers began calling CBS, since they had not ordered the platter. Without those calls, it is doubtful that CBS could have saved the situation the way they did. They immediately called the record back. One puzzled store owner said, "I've never seen a record come and go so fast."

CBS quickly moved to control the publicity damage the embarrassing situation had caused, blaming an unknown employee at their warehouse. They contended that somebody in the warehouse "who didn't know, didn't care, or who was just a goofball, reached in the wrong shelf and shipped out the wrong record."

Shrewd executives in the industry guessed that at one point CBS had planned to release "As Time Goes By," but Nelson had his *City of New Orleans* album coming out and was not looking to cut into his own sales. Julio's manager, Fraile, apparently had come to the same conclusion—but this time attributed it to Julio's hit with Diane Ross not needing the competition. Fraile said, "We certainly didn't want Julio to end up competing with Julio, because then one of the Julios would have to lose out."

Somehow they all forgot that superstars of the magnitude of an Elvis, the Beatles, or Michael Jackson often had multiple hits in the top 10. Just recently Jackson's "Beat It" and "Billie Jean" had gone head to head with neither being hurt by sales.

But Julio would never place himself in Michael's league; they appeal to totally different fans, and Michael's followers are the insatiable record buyers. However, even with the chagrin of the "As Time Goes By" problem, Julio had no complaints.

The tour was shaping up nicely; Julio would be taking his first steps into Middle America. It was risky, taking his show there on the basis of two hit singles and his forthcoming album, but if successful, it would prove Julio's worth in the States once and for all. There was some deserved trepidation in the Iglesias camp. As Sandy Friedman, vice president of Rogers & Cowan, said, "We're not home yet. People in Des Moines may know who Julio is now, whereas at the beginning of 1983 they didn't. But we're far from home."

In the Iglesias camp there was one prime objective—to preserve Julio's image. Every move was subject to the closest scrutiny. The stakes were too high, as he reached this final round in his bout to be the champion singer of the world, to risk on controversial actions.

Where before Julio had been elated to be asked to headline certain galas, now he declined; he was constantly concerned about his appearance. The international artist surprised more than a few when he turned down an opportunity to sing at the United Nations before an impressive audience. The Iglesias staff made light of it, stating "there were some technical problems." After he was replaced by Metropolitan Opera great Robert Merrill, UN staffers confided that Julio had wanted some drastic alterations before he would agree to appear. Objecting to the sound and light systems in the General Assembly, the UN's main room, he had wanted to put holes in the ceiling—for spotlights that would have been more flattering while he was performing.

The same precise care was taken along Julio's tour route. Right from the start the response to an entertainer with two top-10 hits behind him was strikingly different from the interest in a Spanish singer in America. Now his presence excited the crowds at his concerts. And "the Saxons" were crowding out Julio's old fans.

This was obvious when he began his Berkeley concerts, two sold-out nights in the San Francisco suburb. The audience was about evenly divided between Latins and Anglos, but there was no division between the women when it came to their reaction. They went wild, showering him with roses and carnations. Julio returned the favor by stripping off his expensive black tuxedo jacket and tossing it to the crowd. The jacket was torn to shreds in the fans' frantic tug-of-war, and a similar fate would have befallen the singer if guards had not ringed the stage to keep the crowd from grabbing him.

The next day the San Francisco *Chronicle* was kind in its review, saying his "sound was pure and quite pleasant, carried on a steady vibrato that he doesn't overuse. . . ." However, the reviewer did have certain reservations: "After a while all of those tunes sung in various languages begin to melt into one another and sound pretty much the same, but that doesn't seem to bother the millions for whom Julio Iglesias seems to have rekindled romance."

It was not the first time music critics had insisted he was a triumph of technique over natural talent. And Julio is the first to admit, "My voice isn't trained, but I do sing with much feeling. That is my secret."

At the start of the tour Julio's long-overdue album appeared in the stores. A mere five days after *1100 Bel Air Place* hit the racks, it was certified a million-record seller. By its third week of release it was number 8 on *Billboard*'s pop album chart.

Julio was relieved once it was out and much more relaxed after its enthusiastic reception by American fans. But he usually tried to change the subject whenever questions were put to him about its lengthy delay. Shrugging, Julio would mumble apologies about all the problems, interruptions, and travel schedules that had kept it in the studio so long. But he was quick to attribute a fair share of its phenomenal success to the three producers who had worked closely with him—Richard Perry, Albert Hammond (cowriter of "To All the Girls I've Loved Before"), and, of course, Ramón Arcusa. Very reluctantly Julio admitted that one big reason the record was held back for so long was his fear of failure.

Julio Iglesias is honored with a "Welcome to LA" party, in March of 1983. *(Ron Galella)*

Armed with his warm smile, Julio charms the Hollywood foreign press with his wit and candor at an interview in May of 1983. *(Frank Edwards/Fotos International)*

Julio prepares for his 40th birthday celebration at the Hotel de Ville in Paris (1983). The mayor of Paris, Jacques Chirac, presented him with the city's Medaille de Vermeil. *(AGIP/Pictorial Parade)*

Julio receives the Diamond Record from the Guinness Book of Records. *(UNIMEDIA/Pictorial Parade)*

With Willie Nelson
at the Country
Music Awards
in Nashville, 1983.
*(AP./Wide World
Photos)*

A dream comes
true when Julio
duets "All of You"
with Diana Ross.
(John Barrett)

The "Spanish Sinatra" has now made quite an impression on the U.S. public. *(AP/Wide World Photos)*

Usually in perpetual motion around photographers, here he is captured in a rare moment of contemplation. *(Frank Edwards/Fotos International)*

Julio and his three children get some singing tips from Miami Seaquarium's "Salty" the sea lion during a holiday visit. *(AP/Wide World Photos)*

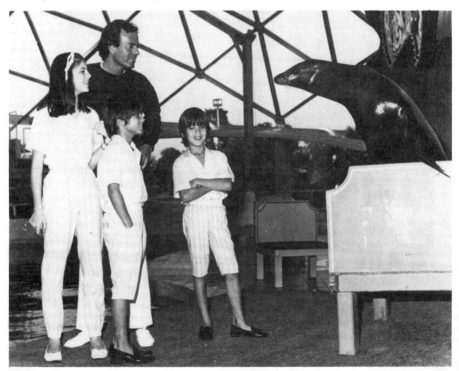

First Communion for Enrique Miguel, accompanied by his father, Julio, and mother, Isabel (1984). *(AP/Wide World Photos)*

With Heather Thomas
at the Annual
Golden Globe Awards
in Beverly Hills, 1984.
(DeGuire/Galella, Ltd.)

Making the scene at
New York's Studio 54,
Julio, as usual, has a
beautiful woman in tow.
(Joe Porco/Galella, Ltd.)

Julio always cuts an elegant figure onstage. When he sings, the whole world listens. (*John Barrett*)

Members of Julio's huge fan club get photos like this to hang on their walls. *(AP/Wide World Photos)*

Julio loves all animals, and is especially fond of dogs.
(Frank Edwards/Fotos International)

Julio on French television, 1985. *(AGIP/Pictorial Parade)*

At the same time, CBS released a third cut from the LP as a single. "Moonlight Lady" was Julio at his best, and it marked his first English-language solo success. It was also the single that best translated into a music video. Bob Giraldi, the director who put Michael Jackson through his "Beat It" paces to great effect, was hired to repeat that success with Julio.

The all-night shooting in a New York school for girls rented for the occasion was turned into a media event. Reporters from the daily papers mingled with TV camera crews and *Entertainment Tonight*, the television magazine show, as they watched Julio make the video of the smooth, softly sung romantic ballad about a man yearning for the beautiful lover who always eludes him. It became a staple video cassette on the late-night shows and undoubtedly added tens of thousands of sales to the album.

Back on the tour, wherever he appeared, Julio's Berkeley experience was repeated. The Washington *Post* said of his D.C. appearance at the Merriweather Post Pavilion that "his concert amounted to a love feast for his fans."

He was a hit in the deep South when he played two nights at the New Orleans World's Fair Amphitheatre. Backed by a twenty-eight-piece orchestra and lit by blue, lavender, and pink spotlights, Julio captivated the crowd.

And since his first concert just happened to coincide with the sixteenth anniversary of his Benidorm Song Festival prize, some of his fans in New Orleans just happened to know the date and presented him with a bronze plaque before the concert. Of course, it made a nice news feature, typical of the kind that followed Julio wherever he—and his powerful publicity machine—traveled. The way his path was smoothed throughout the tour, with almost daily bulletins, proved that Rogers & Cowan was still earning its keep.

For his part, Julio was learning how to play to American audiences. In New Orleans he quickly won the fans' approval by suggesting the Fair guards let in a large group milling outside the gate, trying to hear his show. The suggestion went unheeded since there was no place to squeeze them into the overcrowded theater. Later, security guards came down front to remove a drunk and rowdy young man who did not belong in the front row. But Julio, who knew how Americans root for the underdog, pleaded with the guards to let the man stay. They did and Julio was the hero of the night. It could not have been better if it had been a staged stunt.

And that pretty much summed up Julio's successes in 1984. In a way it could easily have been billed as Julio Iglesias' victory tour. Ticket sales around the country were booming. When Michael Jackson surprisingly was having trouble selling out some concerts, the tickets for Julio's series of performances at New York City's Radio City Music Hall were cleaned out in a matter of fifteen hours, for a grand total of more than one million dollars.

1100 Bel Air Place was bringing in money reviews. Writing for *People* magazine, one of the most influential weeklies, Ralph Novak was very complimentary. "He is not the Latin Frank Sinatra," Novak began, "that the hype would have him be . . . closer to Charles Aznavour. . . . But Iglesias, forty, is a splendid romantic pop singer, with a voice full of texture and character and with just the right hint of worldliness to his delivery."

In New York Julio was caught up in the excitement of the horde of admirers at his concerts. For once, he could sit back and relax. He had met the challenge of America, climbed the highest mountain in his career, and New York, with the toughest audiences, the toughest critics, was his crowning achievement. New Yorkers can be nonchalant, even cool, toward superstars. That is why so many superstars find its streets refreshing. Everywhere else they get mobbed, but New Yorkers merely accept seeing legends walk down their streets. They may stare for a moment, and out-of-towners may let out a yelp or two, but aside from a smile or salute, such encounters are played down. The reason is simple. New York is home to much of the entertainment industry. Pass along one of its avenues, and you are likely to bump into a crew filming a movie or television show. You can find, all over town, top acts in every genre performing live every night of the week. New York comes close to suffering from media overkill. But that is also why every star seeks approval from the audiences and trembles before taking that first step onstage.

Julio need not have worried. But since he is notoriously superstitious, he knocked wood several times, as usual, before hitting the stage. Singing in five languages, he had the audience swaying to his beat, which was sometimes Latin, sometimes pure U.S.A.

The crowd was so congenial that he interspersed banter between numbers, a sure sign that he was finally feeling comfortable in the English language. Joking about his American stardom that did not happen until he was more than forty, he asked the audience, "You people in America—why did you discover me so late?" With a knowing smile he added, "I was so much better when I was younger. At twenty, I could do this for five hours. I used to do everything for five hours then. Now there is exhaustion until the ambulance comes to take me away!"

The concerts were overwhelmingly popular. The reviews for the most part reflected the enthusiasm of the audiences. Rob Baker, writing for the New York *Daily News,* compared him with Sinatra—with Julio in the lead.

"Now all America knows what the rest of the world (including Spanish-speaking Americans) has known all along," Baker began, "that Iglesias has the most extraordinary pop male singing voice since Sinatra—and with more feeling than Old Blue Eyes ever had. He is also an experimenter, willing to gamble and take risks, something Sinatra hasn't done in years (at least not musically)."

Julio's success caught the attention of the *Wall Street Journal* as well. The number-one business publication keeps up with the latest trends. And in Julio they spotted a trend in the music business that bore watching: namely, the growing interest in romantic ballads and tunes with hummable melodies and memorable lyrics reminiscent of the 1950s. Willie Nelson's "Over the Rainbow" and other standards and Linda Ronstadt's *Lush Life* album of golden oldies from as far back as the 1940s had been surprisingly well received, and now here was Julio Iglesias surging up the charts. Upon examination, the *Journal* put its finger on the fact that America was aging and that the kids raised on hard rock were maturing and changing their musical tastes. Iglesias pointedly directed his efforts at the over-twenty-five woman, and his sales said he must be doing something right.

Acknowledging that Julio had come alive to American women in this Coca Cola–sponsored tour, the *Journal* noted that he had drawn overflow audiences from the Concord Hotel in the Borscht Belt, to Pittsburgh, Cleveland, New Orleans, and throughout the Southwest. All six of his Spanish records released in the United States had made *Billboard*'s top-200 list at one time or another, and record store owners believed in him so much that they had ordered one million copies of his first English-language album and reordered another half million three weeks later. Julio was definitely a musical force to be reckoned with.

But the *Journal* reviewer questioned whether he could ever be popular with kids. As one raised on the loud and lively noise of rock, Laura Landro reported that onstage

Julio "seems to drift into a dream, eyes closed, frozen on one spot on the stage as he sings, never involving the audience or projecting the magnetism many soloists do." She also thought the "melodies sounded pretty much alike," but admitted that the audience did not share her views. Midway through his six-month worldwide tour, Julio felt the elation that is part of knowing the job has been well done. Unbeknown to him, the success that he had driven himself mercilessly to achieve was going to be held against him in certain quarters. He would have to fight accusations of betrayal in the coming weeks and go through emotional turmoil.

·9·

A Man Without a Country

Pumped up with his success, Julio was like a perpetual motion machine. His hectic concert schedule just renewed his energy level. This was what he had aimed at, and now he had added the heartland of America to his fan club.

"A year ago someone asked me when I would consider myself a success in America," he told a reporter with a smile. "I told him I'd be happy the day I pulled ten thousand people together in Ohio. In Cleveland I got nearly twenty thousand!"

His success with women also continued unabated. Now even Hollywood stars wanted to be seen in his company. The press quickly picked up on a blossoming romance between Julio and Priscilla Presley, widow of another superstar, the inimitable Elvis. Priscilla and Julio became quite an item, photographed at parties, exchanging small gifts, their every move recorded by the gossip columnists who feed on such new affairs.

Show business cynics, however, hinted that the Iglesias/Presley duo was more publicity stunt than romance. As they pointed out, Priscilla was now an aspiring actress with a steady but small role in *Dallas*, and the couple did share

Rogers & Cowan as publicist. Certainly the agency had been able to get them a lot of publicity. But their friends sensed a definite attraction between them. What may have hurt their chances for a more lasting love was their mutual fear of getting involved again. Each had been deeply wounded by lost loves—Isabel and Elvis—and in Priscilla's case there is the added burden of being enshrined by millions of Elvis's fans who will always consider her the king's wife. The pedestal she has been placed on, against her will, has always made her leery of marrying again.

Then there was the simple fact that Julio could never curb his tendency to flirt. Or his macho image. When he revealed that Priscilla had sent him flowers, Priscilla caught on to Julio's game and admitted that she had indeed done so. "Maybe," she added, "he forgot to mention that he also sent me flowers . . . yellow roses."

When the romance was exhausted, Priscilla admitted that Julio "is an easy man to fall in love with," but indicated he was not the kind she'd marry. Still, it had been fun while it lasted—and it had gotten their names in the papers!

As he traveled through the United States, Julio was amazed at his acceptance there. The response was honest and real, and it came from the poor as well as the rich. The mainstream Americans, he realized, were as happy and proud of his success as he was. This was something new, and Julio exclaimed, "I love America. Here success brings applause, not jealousy. When you ride by in your Rolls-Royce, people don't try to put a hole in your tires."

What this implied about his vast Hispanic audience was not exactly flattering. And there came a time when Julio's love affair with America met the wrath of the Hispanic community. At his Los Angeles concerts his traditional fans again grew restless as he sang his new American songs in

American style. He responded, "Shut up," and laughingly passed it off as a joke, adding that it was a new phrase he had just learned. But the Latinos were not laughing.

The Los Angeles *Times* critic covering Hispanic artists on the West Coast took Julio to task for being "arrogant, impatient, and condescending to Latin fans" at his concerts. The critic noted that there was growing resentment in Latin America of Julio's neglect now that he was trying to ingratiate himself with Anglo Americans. In Mexico a national TV host also scolded Julio for forgetting his south-of-the-border audiences.

The critic wanted to remind Julio that he was breaking new ground for other Latin artists, that he was a social and political symbol for Hispanics living in the United States, representing for "residents of Spanish-speaking nations . . . the seething, emotion-charged aspirations to be accepted as equals politically, socially, economically in relation to the United States."

Julio, it was feared, was trying to Anglicize himself, to forget his proud heritage, to become another homogenized American singer. The writer concluded that "if Iglesias keeps turning his back on where he's been, instead of singing 'I did it my way,' he'll end up with 'I did it the way the market dictated.' "

Even the review of Julio's platinum album reflected the growing rift between the star and his Latin fans. The record's title alone was enough to rankle, since it stood for a way of life completely closed to most of Julio's former followers.

In reviewing *1100 Bel Air Place*, the writer fretted that "far from this ritzy residence, in the ghetto neighborhoods of Latin America, the original Iglesias fan is living in ever-worsening poverty and waiting for that explanation [about why Julio has abandoned them]." He believed that all the cuts between the hit duets "All of You" with Diana Ross and "To All the Girls I've Loved Before" with Willie Nelson are "an exercise in emptiness."

Such criticism was not new to Julio; he had encountered it ever since he had moved to the United States. But that did not make it any easier to face. Perhaps to him this was the kind of "jealousy" he had been talking about, the kind where people try "to shoot holes in your tires" or your career because you are getting too big, too far away from the others.

There was little he could say in reply, but he insisted none of it was true. "You talk about people I have belonged to for many years," he said, "maybe two generations, and now I'm going to forget them? Not at *all.* . . . I can't forget something that is in my roots, my blood, my skin." Then, pointing to his classic Spanish features, he added, "Look at my skin!"

As if to counter these stinging accusations, Julio redoubled his charitable efforts. He headlined a fund raiser for the Cancer Society at Lincoln Center. And he offered tickets to one of his New York concerts to raise money for one of the city's oldest Hispanic service organizations, Casita María, which operates two neighborhood houses for the poor in East Harlem and the South Bronx. Under the auspices of its honorary co-chairpersons, Nancy Reagan and Archbishop John J. O'Connor, three thousand tickets were sold for prices ranging from $50 to $350.

But as 1984 wound down, the Iglesias caravan rolled to an uncommon halt. During a performance in Frankfurt, Germany, the hard work, passing years, and recent criticism seemed to catch up with Julio; his voice gave out. Much as he hated to, he had to cancel the rest of his German tour.

Julio headed for Sun City, South Africa, where he hoped a stay in the sunny climate would revitalize his voice. But a Sun City doctor told Julio that he had exhausted his vocal cords. He recommended that he take an extended rest and sent Julio to the hospital.

When the news leaked out, hundreds of telegrams arrived from all over the world, including one from President and Mrs. Reagan, who considered him a personal friend from the times he had sung at the White House. But after his release Julio felt duty-bound to resume his concerts, even though his doctor warned him that he had been working too hard and that the Frankfurt episode had "just been a warning. The next time could result in something more serious."

Back on the tour, Julio arrived in Paris, where he was hailed as "number one in the world hit parade. . . . 100 million records sold, he has dethroned Elvis and pulverized the Beatles. . . . He has been crowned in Paris," *Le Figaro* announced.

After each performance as many as one thousand fans, mostly women, waited for him at the stage door of the Rex Theatre. It took one hundred policemen to keep the mob from charging the superstar. Once in a while a young lovely managed to hide unnoticed in Julio's limousine and had to be forcibly removed.

But there was no stopping the wily fans. One older woman, whispered to be a titled lady in Europe, managed to get the key to Julio's hotel suite. It was a very startled singer who opened his door that night to discover this woman waiting—wearing little but her perfume! That, however, has always gone with the territory, and Julio graciously escorted her out. When he dates a woman, he likes to do the asking.

Once the tour was finished, Julio returned to his Miami mansion. Even he had to admit that this time he was thoroughly exhausted. In the past year he had finished his best-selling album, made three videos, filmed Coca Cola commercials that eventually would be seen in nearly 155 countries, swept through sixty cities on four continents, taped several TV specials, and been interviewed more times than he cared to count.

Early in 1985 he vowed to take his first real vacation in years. There were no recording sessions or interviews to interfere with his free days. His greatest joy came from his children. Isabel sent them to America to spend their vacation, including little Tamara, because the other children would miss her too much if she was left behind.

Now it is impossible for Julio to go anywhere unrecognized, which he discovered can be a handicap offstage. Restless and bored by the extended inactivity, Julio tried traveling again, from Miami to the Bahamas to Hawaii— wherever the sun shone brightest. Either his children or a lovely woman was by his side. Most of his girl friends were old friends, people he trusted, companions as much as lovers.

But the tabloids were always on the lookout for a new Iglesias story. There would be no respite from the paparazzi or gossip columnists. Julio on the beach in Hawaii with a topless beauty was big news. So was his name coming up in the divorce action of a West German couple. No one was more shocked than Julio when it was whispered that a West German industrialist was accusing him of playing around with his wife. While Julio had indeed been photographed with the lithe, leggy, dark-haired Zohra Zondler at a Munich party, she denied they were anything but close friends, adding that they had seen quite a bit of each other in the last two years. However, she claimed, "I saw his show in more than one city—but we are friends and I enjoy his singing, so it is not unusual for me to have done this."

Nor was it unusual for a beautiful woman to have her photograph taken with Julio, who poses willingly after his shows for his fans. By now, Julio knows it is best to ignore such stories. Denying them merely adds fuel to the rumors.

But in all his ramblings Julio seemed a bit sad. After his unstoppable chain of victories in ancient Greece, Alexander the Great is said to have sighed because there were no more worlds to conquer. In a way that was Julio's trouble. There were no more major countries where he had not reigned as number one on the charts. Now he must plan for his future, but there are few challenges ahead. True, he has made a couple of movies, but it was never a medium in which he felt comfortable. That lack of ability leads him to believe it would not be right "to put that kind of pressure on a director. I am not an actor."

In rare reflective moments Julio confides that there is a loneliness to his way of life. While he is wealthy enough to travel anywhere and has homes ringing the globe, he admits with a certain sadness, "I have many houses, but no home."

Yet he did have the opportunity early in 1985 to go home again—even if only briefly—when he participated in a project very dear to his heart. In response to the British and American rock world's widely heralded and successful recordings to raise money for famine relief in Ethiopia and Africa, the Latin community came together to do the same. With money principally donated by Pepsi Cola, Julio joined some forty-four other Latin stars in an all-night recording session that produced "Cantaré, Cantarás," a single to be sold with the proceeds going to fight hunger.

Named Hermanos (Brothers), the group also planned to produce an LP along with music video and video cassettes for future fund raising. At least 90 percent of the proceeds was earmarked for Latin American countries with the remaining 10 percent going to Africa. It was one of Julio's proudest moments, a chance to reaffirm his commitment to the Hispanic community.

Perhaps this project will bring him home again to Spain. He has roamed the six continents and been a stranger in strange lands. Now, with his children growing up, more and more his thoughts drift back to Spain.

"I miss *my* country," he has been saying. Besides, both of his parents now live in Madrid, although in separate apartments. Truly, his roots are firmly embedded in Spanish soil. If ever he is to find his real, lasting "Moonlight Lady," undoubtedly it will be when he has found a real home. After all the cheering, the crowd does go home. And Julio is tired of returning to hotel rooms. He will never be able to give up his career, but he has come to see that there are other important aims and goals. And new opportunities. He's discovering that it is possible to find a new beginning at forty.

INDEX

A Mis 33 Años, 44, 47
African famine relief, 124
album(s). *See also* records; United
    States album; *specific title*
    first, 23
    sales and successes of, 1, 2,
        35, 37, 42, 44, 47, 78, 86,
        89, 94, 105, 112, 113, 114,
        116
    time spent preparing, 49, 60
"All of You," 99, 106, 110, 120
Amor, El, 44
Arcusa, Ramón, 39, 61, 98, 112
"As Time Goes By," 101,
    109–110

"Begin the Beguine," 78, 83
Benidorm Song Festival, 20–21
Berkeley, California, concerts in,
    111–112
Billboard, 28–29, 90, 112, 116
Brazil, 78

Cambridge, England, 17, 18
"Cantaré, Cantarás," 124
"Canto a Galicia," 10, 35

Carson, Joanna, 86
Carson, Johnny, 85, 86
Cashbox, 104
Casita María, 121
CBS España, 21, 23, 26–27,
    29–30, 31, 35, 37, 39–40
CBS Records International
    contract with, 40, 45
    Crystal Globe Award of, 79
    introduction to U.S. by, 40–42
    Miami base of, 54
    and movie, 54
    and release of "As Time Goes
        By," 109–110
    and U.S. album, 46, 49, 61,
        82, 97, 99, 101. *See also*
        United States album
    U.S. promotion by, 45–49, 61,
        84–86
Chile, 21–22, 35, 44
Coca Cola
    commercials, 107–109,
        122–123
    tours sponsored by, 108
commercials, Coca Cola,
    107–109, 122–123

concert style, 2, 24, 25, 38–39, 64–65, 89–90, 117
concerts, 1, 2, 38. *See also specific city; country*
benefit, 26, 63, 65, 92–93, 121
contests, local song, 20–22
Country Music Awards show, 104
Cowan, Warren, 81
Crystal Globe Award, 79

De Niña a Mujer, 78
Diamond Disc Award, 94–95, 98
Domingo, Plácido, 96
Douglas, Kirk, 83
duets, 99, 100 101, 106, 109–110

"Emociones," 46
Emociones, 47
England, 17, 19, 78–79
English language, 17, 18, 49, 61, 65, 79, 80, 103. *See also* United States album
ETA, 74, 75–76
Ethiopia famine relief, 124
Eurovision, 27–29
Expo '70, 32

Facio, Giannina, 87, 88
fans, 1, 2
behavior of, 25, 32–33, 49, 78–79, 91, 99, 122
Hispanic, 2, 3, 90–91, 119–121. *See also* Hispanic market
older women, 37, 46, 90, 108, 116
Festival of Brassow, 22
Filco, Carlos (Marqués de Grounnon), 51–52

Filco, Isabel Preysler (ex-wife), 33–34, 50, 51, 54, 67, 71, 119, 123
annulment of marriage of, 50
divorce of, 44–45, 50
friendship of, with Iglesias, 45, 51
marriage of, to Filco, 51–52
marriage of, to Iglesias, 32, 33
separations of, from Iglesias, 34, 37–38, 44
Filco, Tamara Preysler, 52, 123
Fraile, Alfredo, 72, 110
France, 39, 122. *See also* Paris, France
Franco, Francisco, 6–7, 8, 37, 40

German language, 35
Germany, 35, 37, 38
Gibb, Barry, 59, 61, 72, 98
Giraldi, Bob, 113
Grammy Awards Show, 109
Griffin, Merv, 85, 96
Guatemala, 26
Guinness Book of World Records, 94
"Gwendolyne," 28, 29

Hammond, Albert, 112
Hebrew language, 62
Hermanos, 124
Hey, 49
Hispanic market, 21, 29, 31, 33, 35–36, 38, 39, 108–109. *See also* fans, Hispanic
in U.S., 46, 61, 109

Iglesias, Carlos de la Cueva (brother), 7–8, 10, 57–58, 59, 70, 71, 72, 73, 74, 76
Iglesias, Enrique Preysler (son), 38, 57, 123

Iglesias, Isabel "Chaveli"
  Preysler (daughter), 34, 38,
  57, 78, 83, 123
Iglesias, Julio José de la Cueva
  automobile accident of, 13–14
  birth of, 6
  called "Spanish Sinatra," 1, 3,
    48, 115–116
  childhood of, 5, 6, 7–12
  competitiveness of, 9, 20, 21,
    24, 35
  decision to become entertainer
    by, 18–19
  and diplomatic service,
    grooming for, 8, 10, 11, 12,
    16, 19
  divorce of, 44–45
  drive of, 14–17, 27, 30–31
  education of, 8–9, 10, 11
  fortieth birthday of, 93, 94, 95, 96
  generosity of, 26, 121, 124
  and high society, 31, 63, 84
  marriage of. See Filco, Isabel
    Preysler
  marriage aversion of, 51, 65,
    66, 87 ·
  music as hobby for, 9–10, 16
  paralysis of, recovery from,
    14–17
  perfectionism of, 49, 56, 60
  personal life of, in media, 2,
    84, 88–89, 123
  personality of, 3, 4, 14, 16,
    42–43, 58
  physical appearance of, 2, 3, 8,
    20, 24, 31, 39, 41, 59
  privacy of, about personal life,
    3, 66, 88–89
  professionalism of, 42, 64
  sex appeal of, 3, 25, 88, 89
  and sports, 9, 11–12
  as superstitious, 19, 115
  voice of, 9, 11, 20, 24, 30–31,
    47, 64, 89, 90, 112, 114
  wealth of, family, 5, 6, 7, 8,
    22, 27, 75
  wealth of, personal, 37, 38, 44,
    57, 124
  and women. See women; specific
    name
  as workaholic, 30, 43
Iglesias, Julio José Preysler (son),
  38, 57, 123
Iglesias, María del Rosario de la
  Cueva (mother), 6, 7, 9, 57,
  72
Iglesias Puga, Julio (father), 7, 9,
  16, 36, 68, 76
  ancestry of, 6, 10
  kidnapping of, 68–76
  marital separation of, 57
  relationship of, with Iglesias,
    7, 10, 68
Israel, 61–62, 65

Jackson, Michael, 101, 105,
  106–107, 109, 110, 113
Japan, 32, 35, 37, 78
Japanese language, 32, 35, 79
Julio, 85–86, 89

languages, foreign. See also specific
  language
  ear for, 11
  singing in, 1, 35, 37, 62, 79,
    80, 94
Latin America, charity for, 124
London, England, 23
  concert in, 78–79
Los Angeles, California
  concerts in, 41, 90, 119–120
  move to, 48, 53

Medal of the City of Paris, 95
Melody Maker, 47
Mexico, 35–36, 120
Miami, Florida
  CBS Records International
    based in, 54
  daily routine in, 58–61
  estate in, 55–57, 58, 122
  father in, 76
  Hispanics in, 54–55
  mother in, 57, 72
MIDEM Conference, 29–30
Miss Universe contest, 46, 61
"Moonlight Lady," 113
movies, 26, 29, 54, 124
MTV (Music Television), 100, 101

Nelson, Willie, 99, 100–101, 102,
  104, 109–110, 121
New Orleans, Louisiana, concert
  in, 113–114
New York, New York, concerts
  in, 35, 38, 41, 48–49, 104,
  114–115

1100 Bel Air Place, 112, 114, 120.
  See also United States album

Paris, France
  concerts in, 39, 122
  Diamond Disc Award
    ceremony in, 94–95
  and Medal of the City of Paris,
    95
  statue of Iglesias in, 79
Perry, Richard, 98, 99, 100, 112
Presley, Elvis, 5, 25, 44, 107,
  110, 118, 122
Presley, Priscilla, 44, 118–119
Preysler, Isabel. *See* Filco, Isabel
  Preysler

prizes and awards, 35. *See also*
  Crystal Globe Award;
  Diamond Disc Award; Medal
  of the City of Paris
  at Benidorm Song Festival, 20
  at Festival of Brassow, 22
publicity campaign, 1, 2–3, 4,
  80–97, 105, 107, 111, 113

radio stations, 79, 100, 104
Radio and Television Festival, 30
Reagan, Nancy, 65, 84, 121, 122
Reagan, Ronald, 103, 122
real estate investments, 37, 40
records. *See also* album(s); *specific
  title*
  for charity, 124
  gold, 1, 2, 37, 47, 84
  platinum, 1, 37, 47, 125
  single, sales and successes of,
    1, 46, 78, 104
  time spent working on, 24, 49,
    60
Rogers, Henry, 81
Rogers & Cowan, packaging of
  Iglesias by, 81–97, 105, 107,
  111, 113
Rome, Sydne, 62–63
Ross, Diana, 99, 100, 101, 102,
  106, 110, 120

San Remo Festival, 26–27
Sinatra, Frank, 3, 5, 25, 116
Sipi, Virginia, 65, 66–67
Smith, Robin, 106
soccer, 9, 11–12
Solid Gold, 96
songs. *See also* album(s); duets;
  records
  foreign language, 1, 32, 35,
    37, 62, 79, 80, 94

songs (cont.)
love, 3, 16, 17–18, 28, 30, 37,
39, 46, 61–62, 99
rejection of early, 17–18, 20
Spain
market in, 29
political and social situation in,
6–7, 8, 36–37, 40, 71, 74,
75–76
television appearances in, 24,
26
tours of, 24, 26, 92–93
unappreciated in, 36, 37, 92

tabloids, 84, 86, 123
television appearances, 1, 24, 26,
29, 85, 86, 96, 101, 103,
104, 109, 113
"Tenía una Guitarra," 29
"To All the Girls I've Loved
Before," 100–101, 104, 106,
109, 112, 121
Todos los Días, Un Día, 54
Tonight Show, The, 85, 86, 96

United States
as coveted market, 2–3, 35–36,
39–40, 48, 77
introduction to, 41–42
obscurity in, 53, 54, 78, 84, 85
packaging for, 80–97, 105,
107, 111, 113

success in, 105, 106, 110–112,
113–116, 117, 119–122
United States album. See also
1100 Bel Air Place
plans for and delays in, 39, 46,
49, 61, 65, 79, 82, 89, 92,
94, 96, 97
production of, 98–101, 102,
112
release of, 109, 112
sales and successes of, 2, 112,
113, 114, 116
video cassette of, 102

Variety, 39
Vida Sigue Igual, La (movie), 26,
29
"Vida Sigue Igual, La" (song),
20, 21
video cassettes, 101–102, 113
Viña del Mar Song Festival, 22

Washington, D.C., concerts in,
103, 113
White House performances, 122
women, 11, 18, 21, 25, 26, 32,
46, 51, 62, 63, 65, 86–88,
106, 118, 123. See also fans;
specific name

"Yo Canto," 29

Zondler, Zohra, 123